THE STATE AND ECONOMIC LIFE

EDITORS: Mel Watkins, University of Toronto; Leo Panitch, Carleton University

2 JOHN McCALLUM

Unequal Beginnings: Agriculture and Economic Development in Quebec and Ontario until 1870

By the time of Confederation Ontario's economic lead over Quebec had been well established. John McCallum shows that the origins of this lead had little to do with the conservatism of the habitants and the church in Quebec, little to do with any anti-industrial bias of the Montreal merchants, and nothing to do with Confederation. Rather the origins lay in the wealth provided by Ontario's superior agricultural land.

During much of the first part of the nineteenth century Ontario farmers were more specialized in wheat-growing than the twentieth-century farmers of Saskatchewan, and when market conditions changed in the 1860s the province was able to use the capital derived from wheat to shift to other lines of production. The Quebec farmers, lacking both the virgin land of Ontario and the growing markets of the northeastern United States, were unable to find profitable substitutes for wheat. As a result, the cash income of the average Ontario farmer was at least triple that of his Quebec counterpar: in the years before Confederation, and this enormous difference had profound effects on economic development in other sectors of the economy.

In Ontario the growth of towns, transportation facilities, and industry was inextricably linked to the province's strong agricultural base. In Quebec little development occurred outside Montreal and Quebec City. Montreal industrialists did have several advantages; yet Quebec industry could not possibly absorb the province's surplus farm population. Ontario's wheat boom provided the capital which permitted Ontario industry to evolve in classic fashion; indeed, Ontario wheat may be a rare instance of a staple whose surplus was retained in the producing area.

John McCallum's analytical and historical account of economic patterns that persist today makes a solid and original contribution to Canadian economic history.

JOHN McCALLUM is a member of the Department of Economics and Commerce at Simon Fraser University.

JOHN McCALLUM

Unequal Beginnings: Agriculture and Economic Development in Quebec and Ontario until 1870

UNIVERSITY OF TORONTO PRESS

Toronto Buffalo London

© University of Toronto Press 1980
Toronto Buffalo London
Printed in Canada

Canadian Cataloguing in Publication Data

McCallum, John, 1950-
    Unequal beginnings
    (The State and economic life)
    A revision of the author's thesis, McGill University,
    1977.
    ISBN 0-8020-5455-2 bd.   ISBN 0-8020-6362-4 pa.
    1. Agriculture – Economic aspects – Ontario –
    History.   2. Agriculture – Economic aspects –
    Quebec (Province) – History.   I. Title.   II. Series.
    HD1790.06M23   338.1'09713   C79-094838-9

Contents

TO CAROLINE

Preface

This book is a work in economic history, but I have tried to make it readable to the non-specialist. The first chapter is a summary of the main ideas, and the last chapter discusses implications for the roles of anglophones and francophones in the early development of Quebec. Chapters 2 to 7 contain the substance of the analysis, and Chapter 8 is an excursion into methodology (together with a brief treatment of the Prairie provinces) which may be omitted without loss of continuity. Almost all statistical tables have been relegated to an appendix, with the principal results given as graphs in the text.

Although Quebec and Ontario each had three different names during the period under study, the modern names have been used throughout the book.

In making its transition from thesis to book, this work lost half its length but, to the best of my knowledge, none of its content. My first debt is to my former thesis supervisors – Paul Davenport, Tom Naylor, and Harold Wright – who suffered through much verbosity without complaint. I am also grateful to John Richards for his useful comments.

This book has been published with the help of a grant from the Social Science Federation of Canada, using funds provided by the Social Sciences and Humanities Research Council of Canada, and a grant to the University of Toronto Press from the Andrew W. Mellon Foundation. My thanks to Enid McBreairty, not only for typing the thesis and the book but also for claiming to be interested even the second time round. I would also like to thank Nancy Lim for assistance in the later stages of preparation of the manuscript.

John McCallum

UNEQUAL BEGINNINGS

1
Introduction

The economic development of Canada's two largest and central provinces has differed from earliest days. From the time of the first fragmentary statistics of the early nineteenth century, average incomes have been higher in Ontario than in Quebec. Since the establishment of the first manufactories, the two provinces have displayed notable differences in their patterns of industrial development. As compared with Ontario, Quebec has tended to specialize in the more labour-intensive, lower productivity branches of industry. As well, the city of Montreal has occupied a dominant position among the urban centres of Quebec to a degree that has never been true of Toronto's position in Ontario; but at the same time, from about the middle of the nineteenth century, Montreal has been surrendering its once dominant national position to the cities of Ontario. All this had become clear by the time of Confederation in 1867, and it is the contention of this book that the origins of these basic facts lay in the vastly superior productive capacity of Ontario agriculture.

Agriculture was the cornerstone of pre-Confederation Ontario. Blessed with the best grain country of North America, according to Lord Durham, Upper Canada had little difficulty in attracting British immigrants to its territory. From a mere 75,000 people at the time of the War of 1812, population doubled every twelve years to reach 1.4 million by 1860. Land under cultivation grew at similar rates, and by Confederation people engaged in agriculture still made up about three-fifths of the total population.

From as early as 1794, when Lord Simcoe recommended a currency based on flour, wheat was the staple product of most Ontario farmers. Wheat was the only major agricultural commodity that could be sold in Britain, and the small size of the domestic market, in combination with the intensity of American competition for such local markets as existed, generally prevented the profitable sale of other commodities before 1850. Drawing on the productive capacity installed but unexploited during the 1830s, net exports of Ontario wheat rose by about 500 per cent during the 1840s, and doubled again to reach their peak in 1861. After 1867 wheat exports fell off rapidly.

A more classic case of a staple product would be difficult to imagine. More specialized in wheat production than the farmers of present-day Saskatchewan, Ontario farmers of the mid-nineteenth century exported at least four-fifths of their marketable surplus. Close to three-quarters of the cash income of Ontario farmers was derived from wheat, and wheat and flour made up well over half of all exports from Ontario until the early 1860s. Thus, until the time of Confederation, wheat was the dominant source of cash income of more than half the population, it was sold mainly outside the region, and it was of paramount importance in Ontario exports.

During much of the first half of the nineteenth century, agriculture in Lower Canada was in a state of crisis. Wheat failed, and there was no commercial substitute. Crop failures became more frequent after 1815, and by the 1830s wheat had failed permanently throughout much of the seigneurial land, which included most of the arable land along the St Lawrence River. In terms of expenditure priorities, wheaten flour ranked not far behind the omnipresent debt charges, but reports of malnutrition, hunger, and even starvation confirm the statistical evidence pointing to a sharp decline in consumption of wheat during the 1830s and 1840s. Quebec farmers could no longer produce enough wheat for their own consumption, let alone for export markets, and, having no other marketable commodity, the habitants reverted to a subsistence agriculture and to a diet based on potatoes, barley, and peas.

The agricultural crisis was due mainly to the unfavourable economic conditions facing the Quebec farmer. Like his counterpart in the northeastern United States, he was forced out of wheat by soil exhaustion at home and by the flood of produce arriving from the virgin lands of the west. Quebec's best farmland had been cultivated for generations, while its more recently settled territory was plagued by poor climate and soil. In both the northeastern United States and Quebec, farmers found it uneconomic to adopt intensive styles of wheat farming when land to the west was cheap and fertile. On the other hand, the Quebec farmer shared with his Ontario counterpart the disadvantages of a small domestic market and intensive American competition in that market. A generalized commercial agriculture based on the home market was not possible in either province before 1850 – and none developed.

Having neither the geography of Ontario nor the growing urban markets of the northeastern United States, the Quebec farmer lived in the worst of both worlds. In comparison with these basic factors, altogether too much importance has been attached to the alleged conservatism, backwardness, ignorance, and other unenterprising qualities of the unfortunate habitant. These characteristics were more a consequence than a cause of the Quebec farmer's economic plight. Had Quebec farmers been more dynamic and less conservative, they might have left the province in greater numbers, but they could not have developed a prosperous commercial agriculture in the Quebec of the first half of the nineteenth century. In support of this contention, one need look no further than the stagnant agriculture across the border in the northeastern United States where the home market was vastly superior to that of Quebec and the land and climate were no worse. Not noted for their sloth, northeastern farmers were unable to withstand the onslaught of western produce, and they abandoned their farms in droves and made their way to the more attractive lands of the west and to the growing urban centres of the east.

Market conditions improved somewhat during the 1850s and 1860s. The Reciprocity Treaty of 1854-66 opened the American market to Canadian agricultural goods and Britain began to import Canadian dairy products. Domestic markets improved in the wake of railway-building in the 1850s and gradual urban growth throughout the period. The new forms of agriculture required considerable capital investment, and the Ontario wheat farmers, having enjoyed record prices and crops in the 1850s, were well placed to diversify their production in the following decade. By contrast, at mid-century Quebec was just emerging from thirty years of agricultural crisis. Naturally Quebec farmers, lacking the necessary capital and saddled with debt, were slower to respond to the new market opportunities.

All this is reflected in the statistics on agricultural production. In 1850 the average Ontario farmer had a value of cash sales at least five times that of his Quebec counterpart, and this ratio never fell below three in the years before Confederation. Such enormous differences in a sector comprising between one-half and two-thirds of the working population had profound and lasting effects on the patterns of development in the other sectors of the two provincial economies.

Until the late 1860s Ontario wheat was the engine of economic growth. Scores of towns dotted the province, and most of these owed their existence to the handling of wheat and the servicing of the local farm population. Agriculture created both the means and the need for locally based transportation developments, while for the country as a whole agricultural exports, which made up well over half of total exports after 1850, provided the traffic and credit-worthiness necessary for the larger transportation projects. Numerous small banks housed the savings of rural Ontario, men of capital were attracted by the growing market, and the financial institutions of Toronto looked to that city's fertile hinterland for funds. All these elements promoted import-substituting industrial development. Agriculture provided the market directly in the form of the farm population and indirectly in the form of the urban population which it sustained. Many of industry's raw materials were agricultural products, while capital, transportation facilities, and other infrastructure were the direct or indirect results of agricultural growth.

On the other hand, an unproductive agriculture and an intermittent forest industry provided a weak base for urban and industrial development in Quebec. And, outside Montreal and Quebec City, little occurred. In contrast to the proliferation of Ontario towns competing with each other by means of roads and railways for the prosperous agricultural hinterland, Quebec towns were few in number, with neither the incentive nor the resources for local transportation developments. Such meagre industrial development as occurred outside the two main cities was of very low productivity, and Quebec's unproductive agriculture offered an unlimited supply of labour at wage rates well below the levels experienced in rural Ontario.

Montreal occupied a special position within Quebec and within Canada. The centre of the commercial empire of the St Lawrence, Montreal stood apart from other Canadian cities. In constructing this empire based on the staple products and import requirements of other regions, the city had become the hub of the country's transportation network, the centre of capital accumulation, and a focal point for immigrant industrialists. These factors, together with the cheapness of labour associated with local agricultural conditions and the power provided by the Lachine Canal, gave Montreal a head start in industrial development despite the poverty of the Quebec market. By the early 1850s Montreal industry showed a high degree of specialization, and Montreal alone possessed large technically advanced enterprises catering to a national market.

Thus, the two provinces followed divergent patterns of industrial development. Ontario industry developed on classic lines as the agriculture-based economy grew. The enterprising blacksmith became a founder, the successful tailor began to employ outside labour, and the printer expanded his operation as local demand for newspapers rose. Markets, capital, materials, and labour were overwhelmingly local. Meanwhile, industrial growth in Quebec was based mainly on elements external to the province. Montreal's commercial base was founded on the production and consumption of other regions, while the city's industry depended on external markets and often external raw materials. The same was true of the few large enterprises outside Montreal which emerged alongside the weak local industry. Owned by outsiders, such enterprises operated large-scale plants importing raw materials to produce a product that was sent to external markets on railways that happened to pass through rural Quebec on their way to the eastern seaboard.

Ontario's industrial growth, then, was inextricably bound up in an organic process of wheat-based economic growth. In Quebec, industry was largely an enclave sector, operating on Quebec soil, but turning to the provincial economy only for the cheap labour thrown up by unproductive agriculture. Hence the agricultural population, which constituted a growing market in Ontario, was little more than a reservoir of cheap labour in Quebec. Industrial growth was internally generated in Ontario and externally generated in Quebec.

Forces of concentration were also at work in the years before Confederation. In Ontario, technological changes and improved transportation facilities hastened the concentration of some branches of commercial and industrial activity in the larger centres. However, by 1870 this concentration had not proceeded very far, for between 1850 and 1870 the share of the five largest cities in the total urban population actually fell, while the number of urban centres more than doubled. In Quebec, on the other hand, the large cities had little scope for usurping the functions of the smaller centres, since there was virtually nothing to usurp.

Gradually, the centre of economic activity shifted from Montreal to the cities of Ontario. The vital linkages flowing from Ontario agriculture – the handling of wheat and the supplying of manufactured goods to the farm population and its offspring – were shared between that province and Montreal. The story of the westward shift of economic activity is the story of Ontario's ability to retain a growing share of these linkages for itself as the province escaped from the clutches of the Montreal merchants.

This escape from the control of an external group, so crucial to the ability of any staple product to foster local economic development, came about for two main reasons. The availability of an American trade route from the mid-1840s broke the monopoly of the St Lawrence and weakened the position of Montreal-based wholesalers and grain handlers. One has only to look to the Canadian prairies or to the southern United States to grasp the consequences for local urban and industrial growth of external control over the transportation and distribution of the staple product and associated imports. This weakening of the hold of the Montreal merchants was reflected in the development of Ontario's major banks, the increasing independence of Toronto wholesalers from their counterparts in Montreal, the independent railway construction initiated by Ontario interests, and the growing drawing power of Ontario cities as 'natural' places to which wealthy immigrants might gravitate. These factors, together with Montreal's failure to attract large volumes of American trade, led to a gradual decline in the city's position as undisputed commercial centre. This weakened one of Montreal's most important advantages as a manufacturing centre.

The second major factor that favoured the local retention of the benefits from Ontario wheat lay in the technology of the day. This point may be understood by reference to the tiny port of Oakville during the 1840s and 1850s. The townspeople financed and built the road that tapped the agricultural hinterland, and the transportation of wheat to the port was handled locally. The town's foundry made the machinery that milled the wheat, and most of the ships used in the export trade were built in the town and commanded by Oakville captains. Consequently, almost all aspects of the process starting with the planting of the wheat and ending with its delivery as grain or flour in Montreal were performed by the local economy.

In contrast with prairie wheat and southern cotton, Ontario wheat ultimately contributed more to the industrial development of the staple-producing region than to that of other regions. From the point of view of the producing region, Ontario wheat was perhaps the most successful staple product in Canadian history.[1]

---

1   A decade ago this statement could have been made with assurance, but now, with the rise of OPEC and provincial governments, the honour should perhaps be shared with Alberta oil.

2
The rise and fall of the Ontario wheat staple

The early settlers in Ontario had little agricultural surplus since only five to ten acres of land could be cleared each year. Nevertheless, immigration was substantial, and by 1812 the Niagara Peninsula and the lands bordering the major waterways were all under cultivation. In the judgement of the leading authority on Ontario agriculture, Robert Leslie Jones, by 1830 pioneer conditions were no longer characteristic of the province as a whole.[1] In that year the population stood at some 215,000.

New settlers almost invariably adopted a system in which three or four acres were devoted to family needs and the rest of the land was taken up in wheat and naked summer fallow. This was partly because the land and climate of southern Ontario were admirably suited to the growing of wheat. New land yielded thirty to forty bushels of wheat per acre, and the average yield of the 1820s was as high as twenty-five to thirty-five bushels.[2] Furthermore, capital requirements were less than in other branches of agriculture, and the roads of the day, while adequate for the annual sleighing of wheat to the lake ports, could not have handled commodities requiring frequent trips.

While these factors were important, the main force drawing Ontario farmers to wheat was the character of the market itself. Small and unreliable, the internal markets were also subject to strong competition from American

1 Jones, *History of Agriculture in Ontario, 1613-1880* (Toronto 1946), 356
2 For more detail on patterns of cultivation, see Kenneth Kelly, 'Wheat Farming in Simcoe County in the Mid-Nineteenth Century,' *Canadian Geographer*, xv, 2 (1971), 95-112; on yields, see John Howison, *Sketches of Upper Canada* (1821; Toronto 1965), 233; William Dunlop, *Statistical Sketches of Upper Canada for the Use of Emigrants* (1832; Toronto 1967), 112; Major Samuel Strickland, *Twenty-Seven Years in Canada West*, 2 vols. (London 1853), I, 259; and H.Y. Hind *et al.*, *Eighty Years' Progress of British North America* (Toronto 1863), 54.

farmers, and until 1850 wheat was the only agricultural commodity that could be exported in any quantity. The internal sources of demand consisted of the military garrisons, the western fur trade, immigrants, the lumber industry, contruction crews, and the urban population. The garrisons provided an important market during the initial settlement of the Loyalists and during the War of 1812, but even before 1800 domestic wheat production exceeded military requirements, and at least after 1820 the cattle consumed by the army were mainly imported from the United States. Garrison purchases benefited the merchant contractors and professionals more than the farmers, and in any case there was a slow depletion of all colonial forces during the 1820s.[3] The fur trade provided a market for the western part of the province, but American imports were substantial by 1807, and the fur traders were mainly supplied by the Red River settlement from 1821 onwards.

A more important market was provided by settlers in the twelve to eighteen months between acquisition of land and self-sufficiency in food. The importance of this market naturally varied in time and place, but on average it absorbed less than one-tenth of the farming population's own consumption of agricultural products.[4] Another market was provided by the construction of canals and roads. This was also a sporadic and localized source of demand, with most requirements other than flour coming from the United States.

A fifth source of internal demand lay in the urban population. Centres with population exceeding a thousand made up only 14 per cent of the population in 1851, and at that time the farming population amounted to about two-thirds of the total.[5] Figures do not exist for the years before 1851, but the non-agricultural population would certainly have been relatively less important in earlier years. Also, especially in the earlier years, most members of this non-agricultural population grew their own vegetables and kept enough animals to provide a major portion of the food required for family consumption.

3 The role of the garrisons is examined by John Philp, 'The Economic and Social Effects of the British Garrison in the Development of Western Upper Canada,' Ontario Historical Society, *Papers and Records*, XLI (1949), 37-48.

4 Between 1824 and 1851 the average annual rate of growth of population was 6.8 per cent, of which perhaps 5 per cent was attributable to immigration. With a farm population of more than two-thirds of the total and a period between land acquisition and production of no more than eighteen months, this market would have absorbed less than 11 per cent (5% ÷ 67% × 1.5) of the consumption of agricultural products by the agricultural population. This calculation ignores imports, which were substantial. See my 'Agriculture and Economic Development in Quebec and Ontario to 1870,' unpublished PHD thesis, McGill University, Montreal, 1977, pp. 68-9.

5 For the source of these figures, see below, Table 5.1, p. 55.

In all of these local markets, livestock, meat, and dairy products came mainly from the United States. Except along the Thames River and along the southern shore of Lake St Clair, Ontario farmers, with their higher costs of stabling and winter-feeding, were unable to compete with the Americans of the mid-west who had access to unlimited free grazing on fine pastures. This competition was so intense that even when the Corn Laws excluded colonial wheat from Britain, and even in the vicinity of Toronto, farmers did not turn to livestock.[6] Local farmers did supply the breweries and distilleries, and tobacco and fruit were grown commercially in parts of the province, but these activities were of little significance for Ontario as a whole. This general picture remained unchanged until the 1850s.

The exception to this situation was the lumber industry of the Ottawa Valley, which provided the dominant market for farmers of the region. The timber squatters who followed the industry up the river and the established farmers of the lower Ottawa Valley specialized in hay and oats, and since these crops could not be transported long distances local farmers faced no serious competition. However, by 1830 the other needs of the industry were met from outside the region. In the rest of the province lumbering remained no more than an off-season activity of the farmers until 1830, and even after that date, in most regions, the industry retained 'that characteristic of a by-industry, a useful part-time occupation, with which it had started.'[7]

In the absence of a reliable home market, most Ontario farmers depended for their prosperity on external wheat markets. For a few years during the 1790s farmers had found a profitable market to the south of Lake Ontario, but this did not last long, as the region was itself producing surplus wheat by the turn of the century. With rare exceptions the American market remained closed to the Ontario wheat farmer throughout the first half of the nineteenth century. It was to Britain that the farmer looked for the sale of his wheat. From as early as 1794 wheat and flour were shipped from Ontario via the St Lawrence to Britain, and until the War of 1812 market conditions permitted shipments of wheat and flour, sometimes from as far west as Detroit, in almost every year. Throughout this period conditions in Britain kept wheat prices high, and the restrictive provisions of the Corn Laws came

6 Jones, *History of Agriculture*, 77, 125-34, 250; Kelly, 'Wheat Farming,' 102, 106-7; Harold A. Innis and A.R.M. Lower, *Select Documents in Canadian Economic History, 1783-1885* (Toronto 1933), 333
7 A.R.M. Lower, *Settlement and the Forest Frontier in Eastern Canada* (Toronto 1936), 42-3. Jones, *ibid.*, provides a chapter on the relation between the lumber industry and the farmers of the Ottawa Valley.

into effect only in 1803.[8] New flour mills were built, wheat acreage expanded, and by 1805 some parts of the province had acquired a good reputation for their wheat.

Following the interruptions of the War of 1812 and two years of poor harvests in 1815 and 1816, Ontario was once again in a position to export wheat. In the pioneer days of the turn of the century annual exports equivalent to 75,000 bushels had been regarded as high, and between 1817 and 1825 shipments to Montreal averaged 264,000 bushels per year. Of this total, 164,000 bushels were the produce of Ontario, and the remainder was made up of American wheat.[9] As indicated in Figure 2.1, total shipments exhibited a declining trend in the first half of the 1820s and then recovered to reach a peak just short of one million bushels in 1830. Although the statistics after 1825 do not distinguish between shipments of wheat produced in Ontario and shipments via the St Lawrence of American grain, there is evidence to suggest that much of the one million bushels of 1830 was produced locally.[10]

Perhaps the most striking characteristic of these figures is their small size. The average Ontario farmer would have exported about thirteen bushels per year between 1817 and 1825, and perhaps thirty bushels in 1830. While hardly large amounts, the lower of these figures was about the same as the average for the Quebec farmer during the peak years of that province's exports.[11] Also, the variations around the average would have been enormous, for the farmer of the Niagara district with two or three thousand bushels of grain in his barn could not be compared with the pioneer land-

8 The basic source on matters relating to the Corn Laws is D.G. Barnes, *A History of the English Corn Laws from 1660-1846* (London 1930).

9 The figure for the turn of the century is from Jones, *History of Agriculture*, 27-8. The averages for 1817-25 exclude the year 1823, for which information on shipments of American wheat was not available.

10 The crop of 1829 had been good, and from the American point of view the tariff advantage of the St Lawrence route to Britain was much lower in 1829 and 1830 than in either previous or subsequent years. McCallum, 'Agriculture and Economic Development,' 81-4. See also Innis and Lower, *Select Documents*, 264-5, for a contemporary's description of the wheat shipments of 1830.

11 According to the census, the total population of Quebec was 95,000 in 1814 and 150,000 in 1824. At the time of the census of 1851, the number of farms as a percentage of total population was 9.1. Interpolation of the population figures and an assumed ratio of farms to population of 10 per cent yield an estimate of 13,000 farms in 1821, as compared with average annual shipments of 168,000 bushels in the period 1817-25. A similar calculation was performed for 1830, and it was assumed that two-thirds of shipments were the produce of Ontario. For Quebec, Maurice Séguin *La nation 'canadienne' et l'agriculture* (Trois-Rivières 1970), 101, estimated that annual wheat exports per farm were about 15 minots for the years 1793-1805, which were the peak years of Quebec wheat exports.

Figure 2.1
Ontario wheat and flour exports, 1817-71

Millions of
bushels

1817 – 49   Shipments of western
wheat and flour down
the St Lawrence
1850 – 71   Shipments of Ontario
produce out of Ontario,
minus imports to Ontario

Source: statistical appendix, Tables S.1, S.3

clearer. Nevertheless, the most important point is that wheat was the only significant *cash* crop, and despite the low export volumes the consequences of poor market conditions were felt immediately by farmer and miller alike. This is clear from the observations of contemporaries during the 1820s.

Because of the operation of the Corn Laws, during much of the 1820s Canadian wheat was forced either to remain in bond in Britain or to undergo a high duty. The effects of the exclusion of colonial wheat from the British market in late 1820 were dramatic. Between 1819 and 1822 the price of wheat in Ontario fell by 50 per cent, and real estate values fell even further.[12]

In 1821 a British traveller made the following observations: 'The only channel through which a regular influx of money took place was by the sale of flour; but this is now stopped, as that article has of late brought no price in Lower Canada; and those persons in the Upper Province who used to buy it up, and speculate upon it, can no longer do so with profit or advantage to themselves. Formerly, the farmers received cash for their wheat, because Montreal and Quebec then afforded a ready market; but things are now altered, and the agriculturist rarely gets money for any kind of home produce in consequence of its being unsaleable abroad.'[13] He went on to observe that the forced collection of debts by the merchants 'would ruin two-thirds of the farmers in the Province.'

Most severely hit by the lower prices were the western parts of the province. The depressed market persisted until about 1827, and in that year a resident of the Hamilton area wrote: 'At the rate that article [wheat] has borne for these last seven or eight years it is impossible for the farmer to become either wealthy or comfortable, unless he possessed the means before; indeed one half of them are in debt, which increases year after year – it has not warranted them in the wear and tear and implements. The present price of wheat in this District [Gore] is 2/6 and on the Thames and the Western District 2/3 per bushel. When it brings 3/9 it pays, and at 5/ – it gives a clear profit of about 1/3.'[14] Clearly the farmers of the day were tied to the cash economy, and a low price for the only cash crop brought steadily mounting debt and the threat of financial ruin.

For the last fews years of the decade, rising prices and export volumes brought a new prosperity. Also, the opening of the Welland Canal at the end of the 1829 navigation season improved access to the market for farmers in western districts. In 1828 the *Colonial Advocate* of York noted the large increase in the number of shops and commented that 'as wheat is over a dollar a bushel [it

12 Jones, *History of Agriculture*, 39-40. Any lack of correspondence between export figures and periods of exclusion is explained by the fact that Canadian produce could almost always be sold at some price, since British brokers were normally prepared to buy bonded wheat as a speculation. T.W. Acheson, 'The Nature and Structure of York Commerce in the 1820's' (1969), in J.K. Johnson, ed., *Historical Essays on Upper Canada* (Carleton Library no 82, 1975), 182
13 Howison, *Sketches of Upper Canada*, 113
14 William Kerr of Burlington Bay, cited in Fred Coyne Hamil, *The Valley of the Lower Thames, 1640 to 1850* (Toronto 1951), 122

had been fifty cents in 1822], and flour daily on the rise, we believe they will all do well ...' A year later, W.R. Wadsworth, a miller, wrote that crops were better than they had been for years and that he could send his customer a large supply if necessary. In 1830 it was remarked in a Niagara newspaper that cash received for vast quantities of wheat and flour must enrich the province.[15]

This prosperity continued for the first two or three years of the 1830s, but the market collapsed in 1834-35. From over a dollar a few years earlier, the price of wheat in Toronto fell to about 35 cents per bushel, not even meeting the estimated cost of production of 40 to 50 cents. Land prices fell by as much as 75 per cent, and it was said in 1835 that 'the inhabitants of Toronto, we believe, never before nor since it was a city, have experienced any thing like the depression in business which this spring has produced.'[16] Under these conditions, shipments to Montreal plummeted.

The second half of the decade was plagued by crop failures in both Canada and the United States. British market conditions were favourable, and the low level of shipments reflected deficiences in supply rather than demand. Indeed, so poor were the crops of North America that Quebec turned to Europe for its wheat requirements. Another unusual feature of the period was the sale of Ontario wheat in the United States. Overcoming the American tariff which had been imposed in 1824, Ontario farmers shipped considerable volumes southwards despite bad crops and despite the political disruptions of those years.[17]

From 1838 onwards, shipments down the St Lawrence rose dramatically and continuously, and Ontario produce accounted for a growing proportion of the total. Most of the shipments in 1840-41 were of American origin, but in 1845 Ontario wheat made up more than half of the four million bushels shipped in that year, and virtually all of the six million bushels exported in 1850 were the produce of Ontario. Exports per farm reached some forty-five bushels in 1845 and eighty bushels in 1850.[18]

Good weather, rapid settlement, transportation improvements, favourable changes in the Corn Laws, and the growth of markets for Ontario wheat all converged to produce the spectacular growth of the 1840s. Much of the

---

15 Edith G. Firth, ed., *The Town of York, 1815-1834* (Toronto 1966), 57-8, 64-5; Innis and Lower, *Select Documents*, 264-5
16 Jones, *History of Agriculture*, 122-3
17 In 1835 exports to the United States were said to be 236,000 bushels and in 1837 sales to the Rochester millers alone amounted to 200,000 bushels. *Ibid.*, 123-4
18 These conclusions are based on a detailed analysis of census, trade, and other data in McCallum, 'Agriculture and Economic Development,' 101-10.

settlement of the 1830s constituted an increase in productive capacity which added to actual production only under the more favourable conditions of the next decade. In the eighteen years to 1851 population almost quadrupled in the fertile districts west of Kingston, while the amount of land under cultivation rose even faster. The opening of the St Lawrence canals reduced transportation costs in the second half of the 1840s, while at the same time the ability of Ontario farmers to ship their wheat via New York prevented Montreal from monopolizing the benefits arising from transportation improvements (discussed in Chapter 6).

As well as the heavy influx of settlers and the developments in transportation of the 1840s, changes in the Corn Laws were a factor in the growth of wheat exports. During this decade the Ontario wheat farmer gained improved and guaranteed access to the British market and a small degree of protection in the home market. Imperial duties on colonial wheat were reduced in 1842, and after October 1843 Canadian wheat could be imported into Britain at the nominal duty of one shilling per quarter irrespective of the British price. Also, as of 1843, a duty of three shillings per quarter was imposed on American wheat entering Canada. It is true that the tariff changes of 1842 also reduced colonial preference, and the repeal of 1846 virtually eliminated it; however, at least during the 1840s, the withdrawal of preference was of little significance from the point of view of the farmer. It was the Canadian millers and forwarders, handlers of American wheat destined for Britain, who suffered from the repeal of the Corn Laws.[19]

Although Britain remained the most important single market throughout the period, increasing quantities of Ontario wheat were sold in Quebec (Figure 2.2). From the late 1820s onwards, Quebec was unable to produce enough wheat for its own population, let alone for export markets. The province's trade deficit in wheat rose steadily, particularly during the second half of the 1840s when the rise in demand reflected not only continuing shortfalls in production but also a modest increase in Quebec farmers' cash income (see Chapter 3). Consequently, the Ontario farmer profited from the misfortunes of his Quebec counterpart, for the failure of wheat in Quebec provided a rapidly growing market for Ontario produce.

The Maritimes were also becoming an important market. With the halving of St Lawrence freight rates in 1848, the operation of the American Drawback Act from 1847, and the adoption of intercolonial free trade in natural products in 1849, Ontario flour rapidly replaced American flour in

19 Barnes, *History of the English Corn Laws*, 250, 252, 276, 298; D.L. Burn, 'Canada and the Repeal of the Corn Laws,' *Cambridge Historical Journal*, II (1928), 263; Jones, *History of Agriculture*, 137

Figure 2.2
Exports of Ontario wheat and flour by ultimate destination, 1838-70

percent

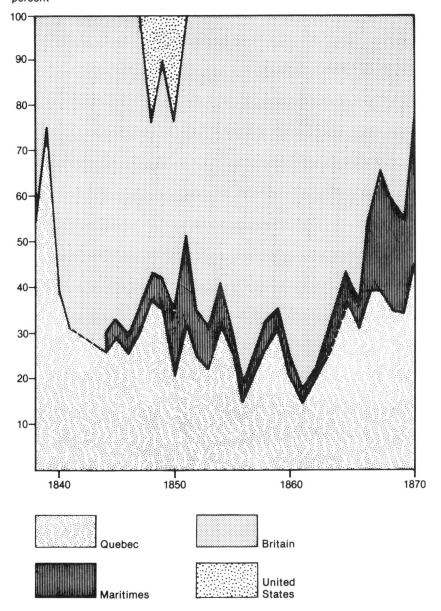

Quebec

Britain

Maritimes

United
States

Source: statistical appendix, Tables S.1, S.2

the Maritimes. Ontario's share of this market increased from 10 per cent in 1846 to 54 per cent in 1851, and in the latter year British North American colonies outside Ontario were absorbing just over half of Ontario's wheat exports.

Higher prices in the United States after 1847 drew Canadian wheat to the flour mills of Rochester and Oswego despite the continuing American duty. Although Figure 2.2 would suggest only a minor role for exports to the United States, the trade statistics on such exports are undoubtedly understated.[20] In addition, flour was shipped through the United States for re-export not only to the Maritimes but also to the West Indies.

In short, after the misfortunes of the previous decade, the fates shone favourably on the Ontario wheat economy of the 1840s. Britain provided a more reliable market and large numbers of her people to settle the province's best lands. Quebec increased its demand for wheat without increasing its supply. The United States provided a market in some years, and, more importantly, the Americans supplied a transport route that broke Montreal's monopoly and reduced transportation costs to Britain and the Maritimes. The settlers themselves built most of the roads, and the St Lawrence canals assisted in the penetration of the Maritime market. Even the weather co-operated with the Ontario wheat farmer of the 1840s. Thus the decade that shook the economic base of the Montreal merchants is seen in a different light from the perspective of the Ontario wheat economy. The 1840s saw not only the explosive growth of Ontario's wheat staple but also a weakening of the hold of Montreal on its agricultural hinterland.

For the Ontario farmer, the result of all this was a modest prosperity. In describing Ontario agriculture at mid-century, Jones wrote: 'The region around Cobourg, that around Toronto, and much of western Upper Canada were as prosperous as any of the newer parts of the United States not directly affected by the Erie Canal, and infinitely more prosperous than those parts of New York and New England where the farmers were suffering from the competition of cheap western produce.'[21] This prosperity, tempered at mid-century by the low price of wheat, was to be eclipsed by the record wheat prices of the 1850s.

The next two decades saw both the peak and the rapid decline of Ontario's wheat staple. Between 1850 and 1856 net exports of Ontario wheat almost doubled in volume and tripled in value (Figure 2.3). In 1853, when wheat

20 The reasons for this understatement are discussed below, pp. 133-4.
21 Jones, *History of Agriculture*, 81, n 38

Figure 2.3
Net exports of Ontario wheat and flour and price of wheat, 1850-71

Source: for export volumes, statistical appendix, Table S.3; prices were obtained
by dividing the value of exports of wheat by the number of bushels of wheat exports

prices were still only moderately high, there was 'prosperity unexampled in the history of the province,'[22] and in the next three years real estate prices soared, the quality of farm buildings improved, and farmers invested in considerable quantities of livestock and improved implements and machinery. The end of the Crimean War brought a return to low prices in the last three years of the 1850s, and this, together with the poor crops of 1856-58, pulled exports down to about the volumes of 1850. Low prices and poor crops, in combination with the end of railway construction and a general commercial depression, resulted in agricultural distress during these years. Worst hit were the farmers in the principal wheat-producing regions of the province, while the farmers of eastern Ontario were scarcely affected at all. A recovery of prices and good harvests brought a return to prosperity for the farmers of western Ontario, and shipments of wheat reached a new peak in 1861.

22 *Globe*, Toronto, 6 Jan. 1854, cited in *ibid.*, 198-9

The recovery was short-lived and the consequences of the low prices and shipments of the early 1860s were described by the American consul at Toronto. In February 1865 he wrote that in the past three years crops in some districts had failed altogether while prices, especially in the current year, had been lower than for many years. During a residence of many years in the province he had 'never known so general depression of every interest as exists at the present time.' A month later he noted the immense emigration and stated: 'Upper Canada has devoted all her efforts to the production of one kind of crop, the wheat crop; and when this has failed, there is nothing upon which she can fall back, nothing either in her manufactures, or the product of her Fisheries or Forests, which can supply the deficiency.'[23] Despite increased exports of other products to the United States, the depression persisted until wheat prices and shipments recovered in 1866. Again the recovery was short-lived, and, with the fall in both prices and quantities in 1868-69, the wheat trade never regained its former significance.

The boom of the first half of the 1850s is easily explained. Population continued to grow rapidly, crops were average to excellent in every year between 1850 and 1855, and the record prices brought on by the Crimean War encouraged farmers to sell every bushel of wheat they could muster. The Quebec market continued to grow, but during this period most Ontario wheat was destined for Britain, either via the St Lawrence or, as became increasingly the case, through the United States in bond.

If the rise of Ontario wheat is easily explained, the same is true of its fall. Following the earlier examples of their counterparts in Quebec and the eastern United States, Ontario farmers abandoned wheat under the twin pressures of soil exhaustion and western competition.[24] It has already been seen that yields had been high – twenty-five to thirty-five bushels of wheat per acre – in the 1820s and that even higher returns were realized on virgin land. By the time of the census of 1851 the average for the province had fallen to sixteen bushels per acre, and only three of the forty-two counties had averages of twenty bushels or better. In 1850 the president of the Agricultural Association had claimed that most of the farms in the old settled areas bordering Lake Ontario were 'worn out,' and H.Y. Hind wrote that in both Canadian provinces 'vast areas of most fertile land have been rendered absolutely unproductive by continual wheat cropping.'[25] By 1860 the census indi-

---

23 United States, Department of State, *Consular Despatches, Toronto, 1864-1906*, 23 Feb., 31 March 1865
24 This process is described more fully in the next chapter.
25 The president is cited in Jones, *History of Agriculture*, 196; Hind, *Eighty Years' Progress*, 53-4

cates a shift in wheat production from the counties along the shores of Lake Ontario to the more recently settled counties further inland. While at that time wheat growing was still the characteristic type of farming north of the Great Lakes, by the end of 1866 barley had largely replaced fall wheat in the older districts of central Ontario. By the 1870s spring wheat was also failing in much of the province.[26]

It might be asked why the wheat farmer practised such a destructive style of agriculture, why, as late as 1852, an estimated 90 per cent of Ontario's fall wheat crop followed a naked fallow.[27] The answer lay partly in the abundance of land, for it was often profitable to 'mine' the land and then to sell the exhausted farm to unsuspecting immigrants who were willing to pay well for cleared land. More importantly, and especially before 1850, markets for other crops were generally non-existent or unattractive, so that modern systems of land rotation were unprofitable.[28] Finally, and related to the last point, when farms 'were cultivated in better, that is, more intensive fashion, the cost of producing wheat was so high that the owners could not compete in ordinary times with pioneers on the virgin soil of the frontier.'[29] As will be seen in the next chapter, the westward movement of wheat production had been a continental phenomenon since the eighteenth century, and when eastern land became exhausted and land to the west opened up, the eastern farmers deferred to the cheaper western produce and abandoned wheat. Only in exceptional circumstances could the easterner make a living by producing wheat in a soil-conserving manner in competition with the west.

Following this continental pattern, Ontario's soil exhaustion coincided with new competition from the American west. When the Civil War began in 1861, farmers anticipated a heavy demand for Canadian wheat in the United States. However, between 1859 and 1863 wheat production in the northern states and territories rose by about 50 million bushels, while American exports rose from 17 million bushels in 1859 to 62 million in 1862.[30] The resulting low prices, in combination with poor crops in Ontario, led not only

---

26 Jones, *ibid.*, 245-9

27 Kelly, 'Wheat Farming,' 97

28 Kelly, *ibid.*, 106-7, describes the marketing difficulties in the sale of products other than wheat. As late as 1854 the farmers selling produce in Barrie had three options: sell from door to door, sell to the storekeeper for cash twelve months later, or exchange their products for goods. On the other hand, wheat received immediate cash either from an inland miller or at the local port.

29 Jones, *History of Agriculture*, 196-7

30 Fred Landon, 'Some Effects of the American Civil War on Canadian Agriculture,' *Agricultural History*, VII, no 1 (1933), 165

to disappointment with regard to the American market but also to substantial imports of American wheat for home consumption. The higher prices and poorer American crops of the mid-1860s coincided with good yields in Ontario and higher net exports, but this was a temporary resurgence. Receipts of wheat at Montreal, mainly American produce for re-export to Britain, fell from a peak of 8.5 million bushels in 1862 to less than one million in 1866, but by 1869 receipts had recovered to over 7 million bushels.[31]

It is clear from Figure 2.3 that there was a close positive relation between the price of wheat and the volume of net exports. The closeness of the relationship is quite striking, with both series peaking in 1855-56, 1860-61, and 1866-67. This suggests that variations in production resulted not only from fluctuations in yields caused by changing weather conditions but also from planned variations in acreage in response to price conditions. After the early 1860s Ontario wheat producers were major exporters only when the price of wheat was exceptionally high, a situation prevailing only when crops were poor in the American west or, of decreasing importance, in Britain.

Thus, by the 1870s Ontario's wheat trade had run its course. From about 15 bushels beween the War of 1812 and the mid-1820s, average exports per farm rose to some 30 bushels around 1830, 45 bushels in the mid-1840s, and 80 bushels at mid-century; a decade later exports peaked at 135 bushels per farm, and by 1871 they had fallen to 60 bushels.[32] Throughout the period Ontario wheat bore all the hallmarks of a staple product, a commodity that was the driving force of the provincial economy. In addition to the opinions of contemporaries already cited, this contention is based on the following observations:

1 The agricultural sector was important: until the middle of the century the farming population made up at least two-thirds of the total population, and by 1870 it was still greater than one-half.[33]

2 Relative to either total population or the number of farms, Ontario produced more wheat than Illinois, much more wheat than Ohio, and in fact

---

31 William J. Patterson, *Statistical Contributions relating to the Trade, Commerce and Navigation of the Dominion of Canada* (Montreal 1875), p. 31 of the 1869 report
32 For 1851, 1861, and 1871, the number of farms was taken to be equal to the number of occupiers of land excluding those occupying ten acres or less. If anything, this results in an understatement of exports per farm. Figures refer to gross exports. Corresponding figures for net exports (that is, exports minus imports) are respectively 75, 105, and 35 bushels for 1851, 1861, and 1871.
33 These figures are based on a detailed analysis of census and other data in McCallum, 'Agriculture and Economic Development,' 63-5, 307-8; see also statistical appendix in this book, pp. 138-40.

Figure 2.4
Estimated net exports of Ontario wheat and flour as percentage of (a) total production
of wheat and flour; (b) sales of wheat and flour outside agricultural sector; (c) total
Ontario exports; and (d) total Ontario exports excluding the Ottawa Valley, 1850-71

Source: see explanation in statistical appendix, pp. 135-6

more wheat than all but the least populated, most western states of Wisconsin and Oregon; this was true of 1850 and 1860, the earliest years for which these statistics are available.[34]

3 In terms of its contribution to cash income, wheat was more important to the Ontario farmer of the 1850s than to the Saskatchewan farmer of today; in the 1850s wheat made up about three-quarters of the cash sales of Ontario farmers, and in earlier years the proportion would have been no lower.[35]

4 Export markets were of vital importance: until the time of Confederation, external markets generally adsorbed over half of total production and about three-quarters of sales outside the agricultural sector itself (Figure 2.4).

5 Not only were export markets crucial for the wheat farmers, but until 1867 wheat was of dominant importance in total exports from Ontario (Figure 2.4).

By any measure, therefore, Ontario wheat was a classic staple product. Wheat was king, but the monarch was benevolent, for the wheat-based economic growth in the years up to Confederation lay the foundations for Ontario's commanding position in the Canadian economy. Before exploring this proposition further, we turn to the Quebec farmer, whose major contribution to the growth of Ontario wheat reflected his own less happy circumstances.

34 Figures on wheat production per capita in 1850 are as follows: Ontario 13.3, Ohio 7.3, Wisconsin 14.0, Michigan 12.4, Illinois 11.1. For 1860, figures on production per farm are as follows: Ontario 193, New York 44, Pennsylvania 66, Ohio 84, Iowa 138, Illinois 166, Wisconsin 226. United States figures are from Percy W. Bidwell and John I. Falconer, *History of Agriculture in the Northern United States, 1620-1860* (Washington 1925), 279, 323, and Paul W. Gates, *The Farmer's Age: Agriculture, 1815-1860* (New York 1960), 165.

35 Levels and composition of cash income are treated more fully below (pp. 45-7). In the period 1965-74 the median contribution of wheat to the total cash receipts of Saskatchewan farmers was 57 per cent. Statistics Canada, *Farm Cash Receipts, 1974.*

3
The agricultural crisis in Quebec

Possibly from 1802, probably from 1815, and certainly from 1830, Quebec agriculture was in a state of crisis which persisted until the middle of the nineteenth century. This crisis, in stark contrast to the booming Ontario wheat economy, lay the seeds of many of the structural differences between the two provinces today.

The forty years following the British Conquest in 1760 were a period of modest progress for French-Canadian agriculture. As in the past, most of what was produced was consumed on the farm, but over the years the farmers came to depend increasingly on the market. By the 1790s they had acquired 'a relish for the manufactures of Europe' which 'not a little contributed to the encouragement of commerce.'[1]

Wheat was the most important cash crop, but other commodities also entered into trade. From at least 1790 American dealers bought considerable quantities of French-Canadian horses, which were recognized as one of the finest breeds in North America.[2] The habitants also exported small quantities of peas, and they supplied barley to the breweries of Montreal and Quebec City, as well as a portion of the food requirements of the small urban population. For their own consumption the farmers kept sheep, pigs, and cattle, which, although of poor quality, compared favourably with their counterparts in the northern United States. In addition to wheat, small quantities of oats, tobacco, barley, flax, and peas were grown for domestic use, and potatoes were introduced soon after the Conquest.

1 George Heriot, *Travels through the Canadas* (1807), cited in Robert Leslie Jones, 'Agriculture in Lower Canada, 1792-1815,' *Canadian Historical Review*, XXVII, 1 (1946), 40
2 Robert Leslie Jones, 'The Old French-Canadian Horse: Its History in Canada and the United States,' *ibid.*, XXVIII, 2 (1947), 125-55. The horse was introduced to New France in the seventeenth century.

The wheat trade made significant progress in the period up to 1774 when grain exports reached a level almost as high as annual production during the best years of the French regime. The 1780s were years of frequent crop failure and poor market conditions, but during the last decade of the century Quebec agriculture enjoyed a new height of prosperity, thanks to the growing level of production which found a profitable market in Britain at the high imperial prices then prevailing.[3] Nevertheless, the extent of the trade should not be exaggerated, for even in the peak period 1793-1805 the average farm exported only fifteen bushels of wheat.[4]

The existence of export markets and the abundance of land were the two factors responsible for this period of moderate prosperity. Apart from years of crop failure or unusual demand from the military, the internal market could not absorb domestic wheat production. Some four-fifths of the population was rural, the market provided by the fur trade was small, and demand from the wood industry was not substantial before 1805. An export market was therefore essential. Until 1790 the principal export markets were the West Indies, Spain, and Portugal, but after about 1795 Britain became the major outlet for Quebec's wheat. There is no doubt that the farmers practised a land-exhausting style of agriculture, but land was plentiful, and production was increased by bringing new land into cultivation as the old soil became depleted. In these early years, then, the techniques used were not effective constraints on agricultural production.

These findings do not apply to two groups that were quite separate from French-Canadian agriculture. A small group of British farmers was concentrated on Montreal Island. Because of their location, they were able to practise an intensive style of agriculture which was admired by visitors from Ontario, the United States, and the French parishes. The Eastern Townships were settled mainly by New Englanders, and in its agricultural techniques and production patterns the region remained an appendage of northern New England. However, less than one-fifth of the province's farmers were English-speaking, and here we are concerned only with French-Canadian agriculture.[5]

Quebec's agriculture in the first decade of the nineteenth century has been the subject of much academic controversy. A debate spanning many years

3 Figures on exports during this period are given by Fernand Ouellet, *Histoire économique et sociale du Québec, 1760-1850* (Montreal 1971).
4 Maurice Séguin, *La nation 'canadienne' et l'agriculture* (Trois-Rivières 1970), 101
5 An analysis of the Eastern Townships in relation to northern New England in given in McCallum, 'Agriculture and Economic Development in Quebec and Ontario to 1870,' unpublished PHD thesis, McGill University, 1977, pp. 204-7.

and encompassing thousands of words has focused on whether the crisis in Quebec agriculture began in 1802 (the view of Fernand Ouellet) or in 1815 (the majority view).[6] The strongest case against any form of structural change in the period 1800-15 is that there was no mechanism to cause such a change. Ouellet claims that production fell after 1802 because of the backwardness of agricultural techniques.[7] No one disputes that agricultural techniques were primitive between 1800 and 1815: indeed, it is universally agreed that this had always been the case. When Ouellet states, without explanation, that after 1800 this backwardness had 'many more consequences than before,' this can only mean that the habitants were no longer able to expand their land under cultivation in the traditional manner. Yet he makes no such claim, and in fact he explicitly dates the beginning of seigneurial reluctance to grant new land at 1815.[8] In any case, whether or not there was a fall in exports depends entirely on whether the peak years 1801 and 1802 are included in the first or the second period (see Figure 3.1), and the same is true of the highly unreliable figures on production per capita.

A more plausible explanation of the lacklustre performance shown in Figure 3.1 is given by Ouellet himself. Describing the habitants' dependence on the weather, he writes: 'Cette agriculture de type traditionnel, dont la prospérité était fonction des nouveaux défrichements et non du progrès

6 Early works containing views on this matter include Jones, 'Agriculture in Lower Canada'; Séguin, *La nation 'canadienne'*; and W.H. Parker, 'A New Look at Unrest in Lower Canada in the 1830's,' *Canadian Historical Review*, XL, 3 (1959), 209-17. Ouellet's views are given in Ouellet and Jean Hamelin, 'La crise agricole dans le Bas-Canada, 1802-1837,' *Canadian Historical Association Report* (1962), 317-33, and in Ouellet, *Histoire économique et sociale*, and *Eléments d'histoire sociale du Bas-Canada* (Montreal 1972). Other writings bearing on the controversy include Jacques Boucher, 'Les aspects économiques de la tenure seigneuriale au Canada (1760-1854),' in P. Salomon, G. Frèche *et al.*, *Recherches d'histoire économique* (Paris 1964), 149-213; Gilles Paquet and Jean-Pierre Wallot, 'Le Bas-Canada au début du XIXe siècle : une hypothèse,' *Revue d'histoire de l'Amérique française*, XXV (1971), 39-61, 'Crise agricole et tensions socio-ethniques dans le Bas-Canada, 1802-1812 : éléments pour une ré-interprétation,' *ibid.*, XXVI, 2 (1972), 185-237, 'The Agricultural Crisis in Lower Canada, 1802-12: mise au point. A Response to T.J.A. Le Goff,' *Canadian Historical Review* LVI, 2 (1975), 133-61; and T.J.A. Le Goff, 'The Agricultural Crisis in Lower Canada, 1802-12: A Review of a Controversy,' *ibid.*, LV, 1 (1974), 1-31. For a more detailed account of this period, see McCallum, 'Agriculture and Economic Development,' 148-59.

7 Ouellet, *Histoire économique et sociale*, 180-8, 275

8 *Ibid.* In a subsequent article, 'Le régime seigneurial dans le Québec (1760-1854),' in *Eléments d'histoire sociale*, 102-6, Ouellet refers to the crisis of the seigneurial system between 1802 and 1854, but in fact all his evidence refers to the year 1825 or later. Also, in Ouellet, 'L'agriculture bas-canadienne vue à travers les dîmes et la rente en nature,' in *ibid.*, 37-88, evidence is taken from 1821 or later.

Figure 3.1
Deficit/surplus of wheat and flour of Quebec, 1792-1871 (in thousands of bushels)

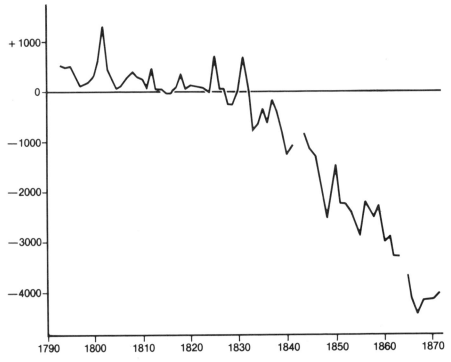

Source: see explanation in statistical appendix, p. 136

technique, dépendait au plus haut point des variations atmosphériques. Qu'une sécheresse, que des pluies excessives ou des gelées hâtives se produisent, aussitôt la misère guettait le paysan.'[9]

Thus, the 'inadequate' crop of 1804 arose partly from an 'unpropitious season'; crops were mediocre in 1805 yet exceptional in the following year; in 1812 damage was inflicted by late frosts and a cold August; in 1814 the wheat crop was destroyed by dryness; and in 1815 and 1816 very severe damage was inflicted by frost in August and September. Also, the Hessian fly was a serious problem between 1805 and 1816.[10] Consequently, while down-

---

9 *Histoire économique et sociale*, 111
10 On the weather, see *ibid.*, 184, 187, 218-21; on the Hessian fly, H.Y. Hind *et al.*, *Eighty Years' Progress of British North America* (Toronto 1863), 56.

playing the role of weather and insects in his conclusions, Ouellet demonstrates their central importance quite effectively.

When to this is added the possibility of a population shift from farming to forestry and the evidence concerning severe domestic shortages in the years of high exports during the 1790s,[11] the case for the continuity of French-Canadian agriculture is overwhelming. Shipments from the west were still insignificant, land was still abundant, and there is no reason to believe that the causes of the periodic crop failures between 1800 and 1815 were different from the causes of the six crop failures of the 1780s.

THE NATURE OF THE CRISIS

The crisis in Quebec agriculture consisted of the failure of wheat as both staple crop and basic consumption item, the failure to find a commercial substitute for wheat, and the consequent forced reversion to a subsistence level of farming characterized by periodic food shortages, declining living standards, and mounting debt.

The gradual decline into the large and chronic deficits of the 1830s, as shown in Figure 3.1, understates the fall in wheat production. This is because there is solid evidence of a decline in the farmers' consumption of wheat, so that if previous levels of consumption had been maintained the deficits would have been much larger. Thus, in 1815 imports were not sufficient to 'liquider la famine,' and in 1816 an observer wrote that 'Le pain et le lait sont la nourriture des pauvres gens dans cette saison de l'année; mais beaucoup n'ont point de pain ; ils supportent une misérable existence, en faisant bouillir des herbes sauvages de différentes espèces, qu'ils mangent avec leur lait ; heureux sont ceux qui ont même du lait ...'

In 1817 it was reported that a high proportion of the people in the parishes in the District of Quebec had nothing to eat and no reserve for sowing.[12] Nine years later an English landowner stated that he had destroyed the habitants' oat-kiln in order 'to prevent the people having recourse to an inferior grain.'[13] Clearly the tendency in this direction was disturbing to landowners, who required a cash crop if they were to receive a cash rent.

The situation worsened in the 1830s and 1840s. Between 1834 and 1846 the journals of the Legislative Assembly contained appendices describing

11 Paquet and Wallot, 'Crise agricole et tensions socio-ethniques'
12 Ouellet, *Histoire économique et sociale*, 220-1
13 H.A. Innis and A.R.M. Lower, *Select Documents in Canadian Economic History, 1783-1885* (Toronto 1933), 50-1

'Parishes in Distress' as a result of the failure of crops and the 'consequent distress of the inhabitants.'[14] In 1833 it was reported that in most parishes of the District of Quebec one-third of the population had nothing to eat, one-third had enough until February, and one-third had enough to last until the next harvest. The main concern was less the possibility of starvation than the inadequate supply of wheat for sowing next year's crop. Farmers had been forced to borrow the previous year on the strength of the current crop, and since it had failed they were unable to repay their debts or finance the current year's seed. Starvation was reported in 1837, and in 1840 the seigneuresse of Beauharnois stated that she had received only 500 bushels of wheat that year and that the 'best' habitants were eating oats and buckwheat. In the same year, Louis-Joseph Papineau reported that people had died of hunger or of diseases caused by bad food, and in 1842 farmers in the neighbourhood of Quebec were mixing their barley with flour to make bread rather than selling it.[15]

The precise extent to which to habitants ceased to consume wheat is unclear. According to Ouellet, the habitant's daily bread consumption fell from two or three *livres* in the eighteenth century to not more than one *livre* in 1823.[16] Another approach is to calculate the per capita domestic supply of wheat (including imports) in the four years for which census production figures are available. This calculation yields a net per capita wheat supply of 4.4 bushels in 1827, 3.8 bushels in 1831, 2.4 in 1844, and 5.3 in 1851. Given a standard consumption level of five or six bushels, these figures clearly suggest increasing pressure on the habitant's wheat consumption at least until the mid-1840s.[17] This conclusion is strengthened by the fact that 1827

14 *Journals of the Legislative Assembly of Lower Canada*, 1834, app. H; 1835, app. K; 1835-6, app. E
15 Ouellet, *Histoire économique et sociale*, 333, 447-9; Parker, 'A New Look at Unrest in Lower Canada,' 211
16 Ouellet, *ibid.*, 251
17 The figures are derived as follows:

	1827	1831	1844	1851
Production (000 bushels)	2921	3408	943	3074
Allowance for seeding	−584	−682	−189	−615
Net imports	−265	−650	+911	+2233
Available for consumption	2072	2076	1665	4692
Population (000's)	474	553	697	890
Per capita net supply	4.4	3.8	2.4	5.3

Seeding allowance is taken as one-fifth of crop from Ouellet and Jean Hamelin, 'Les rendements agricoles dans les seigneuries et les cantons du Québec, 1700-1850,' in and 1831 were years of abnormally high production and also because no allowance has been made for the presumably stable level of demand from much of the non-agricultural population.

Consequently, while there had always been periodic wheat shortages in years of poor crops, these failures increased in frequency after 1815, and from the 1830s production had permanently failed throughout much of the seigneurial land. Furthermore, declining consumption levels reflected not only a fall in wheat production but also a general retreat from the market.

POPULATION, LAND PRESSURES, AND THE SEIGNEURIAL SYSTEM

The natural rate of population increase in Quebec averaged between 2.5 and 3.0 per cent per annum in each of the first five decades of the nineteenth century.[18] In the face of these very high growth rates, the period 1820-50 was one of increasing shortages of seigneurial land. This is evident from the estimates presented by Maurice Séguin, which, if anything, represent an understatement of the pressure on the land. There is also evidence of declining average farm size and a growing ratio of landless to landowners.[19]

Claude Galarneau and Elzear Lavoie, eds., *France et Canada français du XVIe au XXe siècle* (Quebec City 1966), 95, and Le Goff, 'Agricultural Crisis,' 23. This may be an understatement for 1844, in view of the size of the crop. Population and production figures are from the 1871 Census, IV, 95, 96, 109, 144, 155, and the 1851 Census, I, 106; II, 161. For 1827, production figures are originally from Joseph Bouchette, *The British Dominions in North America ... and a Topographical Dictionary of Lower Canada*, 2 vols. (1831; New York 1968), I, 366-7, who stated that the figures related to production 'upon an average of 3 years,' This, incidentally, resolves the contradiction concerning the crop of 1827 in Ouellet, *ibid.*, 332, 336. Consequently, the trade balance figure for 1827 is the average for 1825-27.

18 According to Georges Langlois, *Histoire de la population canadienne-française* (Montreal 1934), 144-5, the French population of Quebec had the highest birth rate in the Western world. Statistics are given in Ouellet, *ibid.*, 197, 272-3, 246, 468.

19 Séguin, *La nation 'canadienne,'* 171-8. Séguin gives the following figures for total seigneurial land occupied (in thousands of arpents):

	1760		1784		1832		1850	
	Area	% of total	Area	% of total	Area	% of total	Area	% of total
Quebec District	470	11	630	15	2200	50	2400	60
Montreal and Trois-Rivières	470	13	940	25	2900	78	3300	90
Total	940	12	1570	20	5100	64	5700	71

From the 1820s onward, therefore, the need for additional land became vital to the French population. However, after 1791, land was granted exclusively in the form of freehold tenure, and the horrors of a policy that permitted nine-tenths of the land granted to remain in the hands of absentees had been described amply elsewhere.[20] Furthermore, after 1826, just when the need for new land was becoming acute, the government adopted a policy of land sales rather than grants. As stressed by many witnesses, the habitants did not generally have the capital to buy land and other items necessary for establishing a farm, so that relatively few were able to settle in the Eastern Townships. On average, only some twenty-one bona fide French-Canadian settlers per year received grants in the townships in the years up to 1840.[21] Given the state of agricultural techniques, these conditions implied further subdivisions of existing farms, a rising class of landless workers, soil exhaustion, and, eventually, emigration.

Fernand Ouellet has argued strongly that changes in the behaviour of the seigneurs after about 1815 were partially responsible for the shortages of land and the general rural distress. The seigneurs increased rents on new concessions; they reinstated privileges such as the *corvée* and hunting and fishing rights which had fallen out of use; and they increased their timber reserves. They reduced the rate of conceding land to force up rents, and they employed various illegal devices to sell their land. They lent money to their censitaires and took them to court when they defaulted. Consequently, to the shortages of seigneurial land caused by population growth and real land scarcity was added an artificial scarcity induced by increased seigneurial avarice.[22]

There is no doubt that these changes did occur to some extent and in some cases. However, the relevant comparison is between the two land

In the latter two years, much of the undistributed land was east of Quebec where climatic conditions were unfavourable, and a good part of the remaining land was either infertile or in the hands of seigneurs who were reluctant to concede it. Further evidence is given in T.J.A. Le Goff, 'A Reply,' *Canadian Historical Review*, LVI, 2 (1975), 165-6, and in Ouellet, *ibid.*, 273-4, 346-8, 470.

20 For example, Norman Macdonald, *Canada, 1763-1841: Immigration and Settlement* (London 1939), 485, and C. Bertrand, 'Concession des terres du Bas-Canada, 1796–1840,' *Canadian Historical Association Report* (1928), 73-7.

21 This figure is based on Bertrand, *ibid.*, 74, 77. Other evidence is given in Robert Leslie Jones, 'French-Canadian Agriculture in the St. Lawrence Valley, 1815-1850' (1942), in W.T. Easterbrook and M.H. Watkins, eds., *Approaches to Canadian Economic History* (Carleton Library no 31, 1967), 122-3, and Séguin, *La nation 'canadienne'*, 208.

22 Ouellet, *Histoire économique et sociale*, 274-83, 351-7, 462-7, 'Le régime seigneurial dans le Québec,' 91-110

tenure systems at the same date, and not the seigneurial system at different dates. It is abundantly clear that even under the higher charges the financial cost to the habitant was less under the seigneurial system than under the freehold system. Joseph Bouchette wrote in 1831 that the seigneurial rents were 'not at all burthensome,' and an Englishman remarked in 1842 that while the annual rent paid in most of the old concessions was a 'simple bagatelle,' even the highest seigneurial rent did not exceed the interest on the land in its raw state.[23]

On the question of land speculation, one need only note that in 1850 90 per cent of seigneurial land in the Montreal and Trois-Rivières districts was under cultivation, whereas 90 per cent of the land granted in the Eastern Townships was held by absentee landowners in 1840.[24] Also, capital was not required to purchase seigneurial land, and this was of vital importance to the habitant. Certainly the market forces associated with urban proximity and land shortages were at work on the seigneuries, but the evidence just cited, together with the habitant's indisputable preference for the seigneurial system, justifies the conclusion that the habitant was impoverished less under this system than would have been the case under the freehold system.

THE DECLINE OF WHEAT

Beginning in the negative, neither market demand conditions nor transportation deficiencies were important factors in the decline of wheat. Quebec had a significant cost advantage over Ontario in terms of shipments to Britain, yet Ontario not only accounted for a steadily rising proportion of Canadian exports but it also provided much of the wheat consumed in Quebec. True, as Gilles Paquet and Jean-Pierre Wallot emphasize, the British market was uncertain and volatile, but this had not stopped exports in earlier years, and

23 Bouchette, *The British Dominions in North America*, I, 376. The Englishman is cited in Séguin, *La nation 'canadienne'*, 180-1. Estimates of rents for ninety arpents of *newly conceded* land, from Jean-Pierre Wallot. 'Le régime seigneurial et son abolition au Canada,' *Canadian Historical Review*, L, 4 (1969), 380 n63, are as follows: 1760 – 3 to 4 livres (shillings); 1808 – 10 to 15; 1820 – 20 to 24; after 1830 – 22 to 54. By comparison, around 1820, the same quantity of land was selling for 2700 to 3150 shillings in the townships. Wallot, *ibid.*, 381 n69. At a rate of 5 per cent, the interest alone on this land would be 135 to 160 shillings. Séguin, *ibid.*, 181, cites a lower price for township land, with interest at 5 per cent equal to 90 shillings. However, he states that seigneurial rents of 40 shillings were charged only on lands near Montreal and Quebec and that rents on most new concessions were between 20 and 30 shillings.

24 See note 19 above; Macdonald, *Canada, 1763-1841*, 485; Bertrand, 'Concessions des terres,' 72; and Séguin, *ibid.*, 202.

market uncertainties were greater in Ontario than in Quebec.[25] Similarly, the waterways of the plain of Montreal had proved adequate for the transportation of large quantities of wheat in the past. Also, with one or two exceptions such as the Beauce, the seigneuries along the St Lawrence extended only a few miles from the river, and if there had been wheat surpluses it would undoubtedly have been in the interests of the increasingly capitalistic seigneurs to build any necessary roads. After all, Ontario wheat was transported by sleigh over much greater distances on locally constructed roads of the most rudimentary nature. For the great majority of seigneurial Quebec, therefore, transportation could not have offered an effective impediment to the export of wheat.

Climate was the major factor explaining the absence of wheat surpluses in many of the newly settled regions of seigneurial Quebec.[26] It was mainly because of frost conditions that wheat production was a hazardous and frequently impossible undertaking on much of the land east of Lac St Pierre. Thus, on the south shore of the St Lawrence east of Quebec City, wheat 'ne semble pourtant guère à sa place dans une contrée peu ensoleillée, à étés humides, à printemps tardifs,' but the farmers nevertheless persisted in growing it, for 'les autres céréales, pourtant plus robustes et mieux adaptées, étaient négligées parce qu'on ne pouvait les vendre ...'[27] Because of climatic conditions, the farmers were denied the abundant crops which might generally have been expected from newly settled land. In 1851, despite the earlier settlement and greater population density in the counties of the Montreal and Lac St Pierre regions, the percentage of total acreage devoted to wheat was considerably greater in these counties than in counties to the east, while yields were uniformly low.[28]

25 Paquet and Wallot, 'Crise agricole et tensions socio-ethniques.' T.W. Acheson, 'The Nature and Structure of York Commerce in the 1820's' (1969), in J.K. Johnson, ed., *Historical Essays on Upper Canada* (Carleton Library no 82, 1975), 179-84, describes the uncertainties of the flour trade from the point of view of Toronto merchants.

26 Bouchette, *The British Dominions in North America*, I, 210, 303, 306; Raoul Blanchard, *Le centre du Canada français* (Montreal 1947), 72-4, 81, *L'ouest du Canada français* (Montreal 1953), 91-2, 153-4, 157

27 Raoul Blanchard, *L'est du Canada français*, 2 vols. (Montreal 1935), I, 154. For descriptions of the climate in relation to agriculture in other parts of the province, see *ibid.*, 27-8, 41-7, 154, 307, 333, and *Le centre du Canada français*, 114, 143, 159.

28 The median percentage of acres under cultivation which was devoted to wheat was about 25 per cent for counties of the Montreal plain, as compared with 12 per cent for counties above Quebec on the north shore of the St Lawrence, 20 per cent for counties above Quebec on the south shore of the St Lawrence, 18 per cent for counties below Quebec, and about 8 per cent for the Eastern Townships. Yields displayed much less regional variation, the medians being in the range of 7 to 8 for all regions except the Eastern Townships where the median was just under 10. Census, 1851, II, 161

The decline of wheat in the older regions of the province may be traced to the combined impact of land shortages, western competition, and soil exhausting techniques. In order to understand this process, it is vital to recognize that the decline of wheat in the east was a continental phenomenon. In the United States the centre of wheat production had shifted from eastern to northern and western New England in the early eighteenth century, to Pennsylvania and the Mohawk Valley by 1800, to the Genesee Valley and Ohio after 1825, and to the mid-west after 1840.[29] Over the years the same pattern repeated itself with dreary monotony: once transportation facilities became available the easterners were unable to compete with western producers, and they abandoned their farms or shifted from wheat to other commodities. The same was true of the efficient British farmers in the Montreal region during the 1830s and of the farmers in the older counties of Ontario in later years.[30]

A few statistics will underscore the similarity of the situations facing eastern farmers in Canada and the United States. In 1851 Quebec imported just under one-half of its total consumption of wheat; New England imported 80 per cent of its wheat requirements in 1840 and over 90 per cent in 1860.[31] The census of 1851 indicates an average yield in Quebec of 7.5 bushels of wheat per acre; in eastern New York yields had declined from 12 to 13 bushels in 1813 to between 8 and 9 bushels per acre by 1845.[32] As early as 1834 eastern New York produced less than half of its wheat requirements. Per capita production in Quebec was 6.2 bushels in 1831, 1.4 bushels in 1844, 3.5 in 1851, and 2.4 in 1860; for the years 1840, 1850, and 1860, the corresponding figures for New England were 0.9, 0.4, and 0.3, while for the middle Atlantic states the figures were 5.8, 5.1, and 3.1.[33] Quebec wheat production was devastated by insects in the early 1830s; in the United States 'the ravages of the Hessian fly and the midge were so disastrous and the reduction in yield so great as to force abandonment of wheat as a major crop in many parts of the East by the thirties,' and 'year after year the agricultural

29 A more detailed account of the American experience is given in McCallum, 'Agriculture and Economic Development,' chap. 4. Most of the information concerning the American westward movement is from Percy W. Bidwell and John I. Falconer, *History of Agriculture in the Northern United States, 1620-1860* (Washington 1925).

30 Jones, 'French-Canadian Agriculture,' 117, and *History of Agriculture in Ontario, 1613-1880* (Toronto 1946), 245-6

31 Bidwell and Falconer, *History of Agriculture*, 311

32 David M. Ellis, *Landlords and Farmers in the Hudson-Mohawk Region, 1790-1850* (New York 1967), 187-9

33 United States census figures are taken from Bidwell and Falconer, *History of Agriculture*.

press [in New York] carried reports of the destruction of wheat crops by the midge, the rust, or the fly.'[34]

Both regions, then, experienced exactly the same difficulties: declining yields due to the continuous cropping of wheat, falling prices associated with increased western supplies,[35] rising land prices and rents, and attacks from various destructive insects. Both regions adopted the same solution to these problems: they ceased to grow wheat as a major product and became net importers of breadstuffs. Indeed, as compared with the Mohawk Valley and other parts of the eastern United States, Quebec's circumstances were decidedly inferior. Its climate, as we have seen, was much less suitable for the growing of wheat, and its greater distance from European markets and shorter shipping season put it at a disadvantage relative to the lands along the Mohawk River, although in some periods this drawback would have been offset by colonial preference. Quebec had grown wheat since the seventeenth century. What is surprising, then, is not that wheat production in Quebec failed, but rather that its farmers continued to grow it for as long as they did. As will be seen presently, this persistence was mainly a reflection of the absence of attractive alternatives.

What does all this imply for Ouellet's view[36] that the failure of wheat was due to the inability or unwillingness of the habitants to adopt modern methods of agriculture? Could they not have adopted a more intensive style of wheat farming in order to counter the effects of soil exhaustion? The simple answer is that extensive wheat farming was cheaper than intensive wheat farming, and as long as the former could be practised in the west the latter was only a paying proposition in the east if the cost of transportation outweighed the additional costs of intensive farming. This was rarely the case in practice, and it was never the case when there were poor market conditions for the products which formed part of the cycle of intensive wheat farming. These contentions are supported by the experience of the eastern United States and Ontario.

It has already been observed that 90 per cent of Ontario's fall wheat in 1852 followed a naked fallow. In the same year a reliable source estimated that one-twelfth of all New York farmers improved their lands, one-fourth prevented deterioration, and the rest 'skinned' the land, damaging it to the

34 Paul W. Gates, *The Farmer's Age: Agriculture, 1815-1860* (New York 1960), 164; Ellis, *Landlords and Farmers*, 188
35 Price trends for Philadelphia, Quebec, and London are given in Le Goff, 'Agricultural Crisis,' 14.
36 This view is given in Ouellet, *Histoire économique et sociale*, 187-8, 252-6.

extent of $3 per acre each year.[37] Not noted for their ignorance, the farmers of Ontario and New York nevertheless practised a soil-destroying method of wheat growing.

In both the United States and Ontario land availability was only one of the factors that encouraged soil-exhausting practices. An additional factor was the 'lack of capital [which] prevented many farmers from making the necessary improvements and acquiring cows and sheep which successful farming required.' Also, the fact that wheat was frequently the only saleable product was a serious impediment to crop rotation. This was the case in Ontario, and in the early years in eastern New York the farmers' 'need for cash was too urgent to be delayed' by crop rotation.[38] Furthermore, eastern wheat production in the United States declined despite the rapid growth in urban markets, which permitted the sale of crops complementary to intensive wheat production and the sale of dairy products which would have ensured a supply of manure. The development of the urban market, which was a necessary condition of a non-exhausting system of wheat growing, was not sufficient to stem the decline of eastern production in the face of western competition.

How much more serious were the problems of the farmer of French Canada, in comparison with whom the eastern American farmer had abundant capital and an enormous urban market; and how unreasonable to ascribe the habitant's inability to compete with western wheat to his personal shortcomings when others much better placed than he had also bowed to the challenge of western wheat. Indeed, soil-exhausting techniques are a general characteristic of dependence on a single crop, and this is not the only case in which the practitioners have been blamed for a pattern of behaviour which is properly attributable to an environment over which the practitioners exert no control. Thus, referring to the agriculture of the American South, Avery Odelle Craven concluded that 'the destructive practices of the Old South were in fact, in the beginning merely the normal product of frontier conditions,' that these practices 'were continued under the influence of markets and government,' and that 'the blame for so wide-spread destruction cannot be placed upon any inherent careless, shiftless, or easy-going character so often ascribed to the men of the Old South,'[39] The same comment applies to

37 Ellis, *Landlords and Farmers*, 90
38 *Ibid.*, 156, 90. For Ontario, see Kenneth Kelly, 'Wheat Farming in Simcoe County in the Mid-Nineteenth Century,' *Canadian Geographer*, xv, 2 (1971), 95-112, and Jones, *History of Agriculture*, 196-7.
39 Craven, *Soil Exhaustion as a Factor in the Agricultural History of Virginia and Maryland, 1606-1860* (Gloucester, Mass. 1965), 162-4

the ignorant, conservative, and luxury-loving character so often ascribed to the habitants of Quebec.

SUBSTITUTES FOR WHEAT

Clearly the farmers of the seigneuries found substitutes for wheat, for they shifted production to those items that satisfied their own requirements for food and clothing. The question is why they did not shift to commodities that could be sold on the market and why, in particular, many of the requirements of the non-agricultural population came to be provided by imports.

Once again comparison with the eastern United States is illuminating. In 1870, the first year for which American data are available, the agricultural working population accounted for 13 per cent of the total working population in Massachusetts, 23 per cent in Connecticut, and 25 per cent in New York and Pennsylvania. In the same year, the agricultural sector accounted for just over half of the working population of Quebec. Thus, the internal market facing the average New York farmer was approximately triple that facing his Quebec counterpart in 1870. Similarly, in 1850 the relative importance of the urban population was about three times as great in the northeastern United States as in Quebec.[40]

The ability of the farmers of the eastern United States to find commodities in which they could compete with westerners was dependent on this urban growth. The easterners turned to hay, dairy products, and market gardening, areas in which bulk or perishability prevented effective western competition. The basis of their viability was market proximity, and, in the words of P.W. Bidwell and J.I. Falconer, '... whenever a branch of agricultural production, such as wheat, wool or beef, proved profitable in the West and poured its supplies into the eastern markets, it became necessary for the eastern farmer to find some other line of production, and, *fortunately for the eastern farmer, the development of urban population made this possible.*'

Despite the rapid growth of internal markets, rural depopulation was a fact of life in the eastern states. Between 1790 and 1820 emigration from Connecticut, Massachusetts, and Rhode Island exceded the total population of 1790, and in these same states the population of the agricultural districts declined in absolute numbers between 1810 and 1840.[41] After the initial periods of

40 United States, Ninth Census, 1870, I, 670-1. For Quebec, an analysis of the relative importance of the agricultural population is given in McCallum, 'Agriculture and Economic Development,' 187-92, 307-8; see also *ibid.*, 133-4.

41 Bidwell and Falconer, *History of Agriculture*, 452 (emphasis added), 200; Bidwell, 'Rural Economy in New England at the Beginning of the 19th Century,' *Transactions of the Con-*

settlement, Vermont, New Hampshire, and Maine were unable to retain the natural increase in their population. By 1860 the population of New Hampshire was only 35 per cent of what it would have been if it had grown at the natural rate of increase since 1790. For Vermont and Maine comparable figures are 57 and 100 per cent.[42] By 1825 'eastern New York was contributing its own sons to the westward-flowing stream,' and even in the Genesee Valley of western New York the agricultural population was stable or declining after about 1840.[43]

We find, then, that despite the fantastic growth of towns the eastern agricultural population was stagnant or declining. On the whole, eastern farmers found the deterrent of western competition to be more potent than the market stimulus of urban growth, and so they left their farms for the greater attractions of the cities and the west.

It has already been observed that Quebec's internal market was much smaller than that of the American northeast. The weight of the evidence suggests that 70 per cent is a conservative estimate of the ratio of the farming population to the total population of Quebec in 1851.[44] Of the remaining 30 per cent, half lived in centres with population exceeding one thousand, and the rest of the population, scattered throughout rural Quebec, satisfied its own food requirements to varying degrees. For earlier years information is fragmentary. However, William Evans, one of Quebec's leading agricultural authorities, stated in 1836 that 85 per cent of the population 'belong exclusively to the agricultural class,' and Séguin gave the same figure for 1820.[45]

In some areas the habitants did satisfy the needs of this local market. Those in the immediate vicinity of Quebec City responded to the growth in demand occasioned by the expansion of the timber trade, and in general the farmers continued to supply the towns and shanties with oats, peas, and

necticut Academy of Arts and Sciences, xx (April 1916), 386-8, reprinted by August M. Kelly (Clifton, NJ 1972)

42 Population growth rates by decade are from Bidwell and Falconer, ibid., 199, 279; natural rates of increase for the United States are derived from Conrad and Irene B. Taeuber, The Changing Population of the United States, Census Monograph Series (New York 1958), 5, 294

43 Ellis, Landlords and Farmers, 156; Neil Adams McNall, An Agricultural History of the Genessee Valley, 1790-1860 (Philadelphia 1952), 232

44 This conclusion is reached in McCallum, 'Agriculture and Economic Development,' 187-92 after close analysis of the census data and other sources. Some 3 to 10 per cent of farmers and farm workers would have received a significant supplement to their incomes from seasonal work in shipbuilding and in the timber trade. See also pp. 138-40 in this book.

45 Evans, Supplementary Volume to a Treatise on the Theory and Practice of Agriculture (Montreal 1836), 72: Séguin, La nation 'canadienne', 74

potatoes and the distilleries and breweries with rye and barley. The French-Canadian horse retained its good reputation, and exports to the United States and Ontario were maintained throughout the first half of the nineteenth century.[46]

Because of the limited size of the market, these articles were sold only in small quantities, and their low value in relation to bulk rendered their marketing uneconomic in most parts of the province. As Evans wrote in 1850: 'A large proportion of the arable land of every farm might have been appropriated to the growing of wheat, but since the failure of that crop, all the land is employed in producing crops that can only be consumed in Canada. Hence, the market must be glutted with this description of produce.'[47]

Furthermore, not only was the market small in relation to productive capacity but it also tended to be unstable. Commodities such as oats, for which the highly volatile timber trade was the major market, were subject to large and sudden changes in price; but despite these unfavourable circumstances habitants brought their oats and barley to Montreal from distances as great as one hundred miles. Thus, in the case of crops other than wheat, the crisis was one of inadequate demand, not supply.

It was in the area of livestock (other than horses) and livestock products that the habitants were unable or unwilling to compete with imports. Ouellet presents estimates of net imports of such products for various time periods beginning in 1818. While he uses the data to stress the habitants' inability to supply the domestic market, a more interesting point is the very low volumes of imports represented by the figures. Taking maximum estimates of the annual volumes, the annual value of imports at 1850 prices was about $345,000. This is equivalent to about 350,000 bushels of wheat, or just over 5 per cent of total shipments from Ontario in 1850. It works out to less than five dollars per farm, which is less than one-third of the average Quebec farmer's cash income from wheat exports at the beginning of the century.[48]

46 Blanchard, *Le centre du Canada français*, 81-2, *L'ouest du Canada français* (Montreal 1953), 91; Jones, 'French-Canadian Agriculture,' 118, 120; Parker, 'A New Look at Unrest in Lower Canada,' 215; Ouellet, *Histoire économique et sociale*, 341, 'L'agriculture bas-canadienne,' 69, 71

47 Cited in Jones, *ibid.*, 118

48 Ouellet's figures, *Histoire économique et sociale*, 343-5, 423, 610-14, were supplemented with information from I.D. Andrews, *Report on the Trade, Commerce, and Resources of the British North American Colonies* ... United States, 31st Congress, 2nd session, executive document no 23 (Washington 1851), 180, 282-3, 286. Prices are from K.W. Taylor and H. Mitchell, *Statistical Contributions to Canadian Economic History* (Toronto 1931); I.D. Andrews, *Report on the Trade and Commerce of the British North American Colonies and upon the Trade of the Great Lakes and Rivers*, United States, 32nd Congress, 1st session,

Consequently, if the figures are accurate (and Ouellet expresses no reservations), then even a total elimination of imports would have had a barely perceptible effect on the income and production levels of French-Canadian agriculture. Here, then, is another indication of the small size of the domestic market.

The size of the market was not the only reason for the habitants' failure to develop a commercial livestock industry. As in the United States, western competition was a major factor, for in the words of Jones:

After 1815, Montreal and Quebec were great exporters of the agricultural surplus of the basin of the Great Lakes. The consequence was that the foodstuffs they consumed were more easily obtained from the westward than from any but the most adjacent parts of Lower Canada. Thus, the lumber shanties of the Ottawa valley came to be supplied through Montreal with Cincinnati pork, the butchers of Montreal and Quebec with Vermont cattle, and the grocers of the towns of Lower Canada with Ohio and Vermont cheese. The British farmers around Montreal did get a share of the local livestock market, and so did the inhabitants of the Eastern Townships, but both of these groups found difficulty in competing with American imports ... Under these circumstances, when the relatively efficient British farmers of Lower Canada could not meet American competition, it would have been unreasonable to expect any appreciable growth in livestock raising among the habitants; and none took place.[49]

Americans were especially prone to sell their cattle in Canada when their home market was glutted, and this dumping of imports naturally created market instability. The *British American Cultivator* remarked in 1842 that 'farmers are not disposed to stall feed cattle in consequence of the extreme uncertainty of the [Montreal] market. A large supply of fat cattle and sheep may come in from a foreign country at any time, and reduce the price so much, as to leave the farmer scarcely any remuneration for the extra food and trouble of stall feeding.'[50] Indeed, in the face of the American competition and the falling prices of the 1840s, it was said that the English farmers were operating at a loss. William Evans stated that livestock were selling at a 50 per cent loss, and other English farmers echoed this view. This was so

executive document no 136 (1852-53), 476; and Census, 1851, I, xxvi. A full analysis is given in McCallum, 'Agriculture and Economic Development,' 195-8.

49 Jones, 'French-Canadian Agriculture,' 121-2

50 Cited in Robert Leslie Jones, 'The Canadian Agricultural Tariff of 1843,' *Canadian Journal of Economics and Political Science*, VII, 4 (1941), 533

despite the inauguration of the tariff of 1843, for which English farmers in both provinces had long campaigned.[51]

It was not difficult for the habitants to produce coarse grains for the market or to sell the horses that had been raised in a manner acceptable to the market for decades. On the other hand, they would have required considerable capital to embark on the commercial production of other forms of livestock and livestock products. Their livestock, cheese, butter, wool, and meat were frequently unacceptable in the urban market, though presumably satisfactory for their own use. The wool from their sheep was too coarse, their beef was considered decidedly inferior, their cheese was referred to as 'stinking cheese,' and only one region, Kamouraska, had developed a reputation for butter. Their pastures were generally deficient, and their livestock, again with the exception of horses, were inadequately sheltered and fed in the winter.[52] Consequently, any venture into commercial production would have involved considerable expenditure for better breeds of livestock, better shelter during the winter, and more abundant supplies of feed for the animals.

The 'improving farmers' of Ontario were a minority who were able to practise mixed farming only because they had brought a substantial amount of capital into Ontario with them.[53] At a time of a general capital scarcity in Ontario, it is hardly surprising that the habitants lacked the means for a shift to commercial livestock-raising. After all, the period was one of failure of the only significant cash crop, rising seigneurial charges, and a chronic state of indebtedness. In relatively good times debt obligations prevented the purchase of new livestock, while in bad times stock had to be reduced. Under circumstances in which farmers had to use their savings to buy flour[54] or to forego the consumption of that article altogether, it is clear that they were in no position to enter into the commercial livestock industry. When we add to this the facts that the English-speaking farmers were losing money, that the size of the market was very small, and that in many branches of the industry eastern American farmers could not compete with western produce in their own much larger local markets, it is obvious that any generalized participation by the habitants was not only financially impossible, but would have been an unmitigated disaster for all concerned.

Thus, while the decline of wheat was the inevitable consequence of the westward movement of agriculture, the failure to find a commercial substi-

51 Ouellet and Hamelin, 'Les rendements agricoles,' 113; also relevant are Jones, *ibid.*, and Ouellet, *Histoire économique et sociale*, 460-1.
52 Jones, 'French-Canadian Agriculture,' 119-21
53 Kelly, 'Wheat Farming,' 102
54 Ouellet, *Histoire économique et sociale*, 340

tute is adequately explained by the market situation. The Quebec farmer of the first half of the nineteenth century lived in the worst of all worlds. Facing the same flood of western produce as his American counterpart, he lacked the large and growing internal markets which saved some but by no means all of the farmers of the northeastern United States. Facing the same foreign competition and limited home market as the Ontario farmer, he was unable to produce wheat for export.

In this hopeless economic environment the habitant's poor farming practices lose both their mystery and their importance. The American experience demonstrates the crucial role of favourable market conditions in the improvement of agricultural techniques; for in the words of Bidwell and Falconer the growth of the market 'did what all the exhortations of agricultural societies and publicists had failed to do. It stimulated increased production, better tillage,' and improvement of livestock.'[55] More important, however, even if Quebec's agricultural societies had enjoyed a greater success in disseminating modern farming methods, the rewards from such improvements would have been meagre. With better techniques the habitants might have been able to hang on to wheat for a few more years, or they might even have increased their share of the home market. These would have been but marginal gains, for the most important factors shaping Quebec agriculture were beyond the control of publicist and farmer alike.

THE CRISIS AND THE FARMER

For the habitant, the crisis meant inadequate diet, poor health, chronic debt, and emigration. The switch from wheat to other grains as the basis of consumption and the periodic food shortages have already been discussed, and H.C. Pentland has presented evidence of the declining state of health which resulted from these conditions.[56] Concerning debt, reference has been made to the habitants' inability to repay loans incurred for the purhcase of seed after a series of bad crops. There is much additional evidence of the pervasive and chronic nature of habitant indebtedness.

In his otherwise 'pleasant picture' of the standard of living on the Mille Isles seigneury, Stanford W. Reid emphasized the large numbers of promissory notes or obligations contained in the notarial *greffes* from the earliest days of the seigneury. Usually debts were first contracted for the purchase of

55 Bidwell and Falconer, *History of Agriculture*, 198
56 Pentland, 'Labour and the Development of Industrial Capitalism in Canada,' unpublished PHD thesis, University of Toronto, 1960, pp. 150-1

seed and equipment, but during the 1840s there was an increasing number of cash loans. The habitants were frequently seven to ten years behind in their payment of *cens et rentes*, and the seigneurs turned over the collection of these rents to merchants who forced the sale of land belonging to delinquent debtors. A common practice among the local money-lenders was to convert a portion of each loan to a pension payable by the debtors every year until the death of the creditors or their wives. Such practices led to perpetual indebtedness among the habitants, and Reid concluded that 'by 1850, a great many of the habitants must have been in the clutches of such local loan sharks.'[57]

French-Canadian emigration had taken place as early as 1808,[58] but it was during the 1840s that the movement reached significant proportions. A select committee of the Legislative Assembly in 1849 estimated that emigration had amounted to an annual average of four thousand in the past five years, of which the agricultural class had accounted for two-thirds.[59] The failure of commercial agriculture, in combination with high population growth and impediments to new settlement, created conditions in which emigration was the only alternative for a significant and rising proportion of the population.

Nevertheless, the emigration of this period was on a modest scale in comparison with the experience of the northeastern United States, and it is in this area, rather than in the area of agricultural techniques, that social factors must form an important part of the explanation. In legend if not in fact, the westward movement symbolized adventure and even romance for the sons of New England. For French Canada, on the other hand, emigration was a matter of grave national concern. American farmers could never have suffered as the habitants did, for they would have moved west long before that point was reached. In Quebec the joint effect of this limited emigration and the agricultural crisis was a large pool of surplus labour, which, making itself available at very low wages, was to have a major impact on the pattern of growth of the Quebec economy.

57 Reid, 'The Habitant's Standard of Living on the Signeurie des Mille Isles, 1820-50,' *Canadian Historical Review*, XXVIII, 3 (1947), 276-7
58 Marcus Lee Hansen, *The Mingling of the Canadian and American Peoples* (New Haven 1940), 123-4
59 *Journals of the Legislative Assembly of Canada*, app. AAAAA, p. 3

4

Agricultural transformation in Quebec and Ontario, 1850-70

The two decades between 1850 and 1870 saw a transformation of agriculture in both provinces. In Ontario a diversified pattern of production replaced the monoculture of the wheat economy, while in Quebec the retreat from the market was halted and reversed as the agricultural sector began to recover. In the course of these structrual transformations, as the farmers of the two provinces began to operate in the same markets and to respond, albeit in different ways, to the same forces, the worlds of Quebec and Ontario agriculture began to converge; and it is therefore appropriate to treat the two provinces together.

The basic information concerning cash income from agriculture is given in Figure 4.1. The derivation of this information is described in detail in the statistical appendix; in general, production figures are derived from the census, and estimates of cash income are based on a commodity by commodity examination of the census, the Trade and Navigation Returns, and evidence concerning the size and nature of the home market. For reasons given in the appendix, the figures tend, if anything, to overstate the relative position of Quebec farmers. The gross value of agricultural production was about half as great in Quebec as in Ontario, and the average Quebec farmer produced about two-thirds as much as his Ontario counterpart. However, these figures include the total value of commodities such as hay and oats which were used mainly as feed for livestock. Since these two commodities were much more important to Quebec than to Ontario (accounting for averages of respectively 45 per cent and 27 per cent of total production), the above figures understate Ontario's lead in terms of net output of agricultural goods, or value added. From the perspective of this book, *cash* income is much more important than either gross or net output. This is because we are concerned with the linkages between agriculture and the rest of the economy, and these linkages

Figure 4.1
Estimated cash income from agriculture, 1851-70

1 Aggregate income

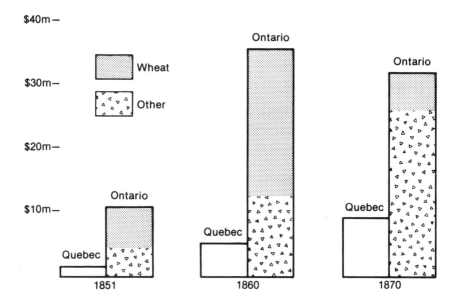

2 Income per farm

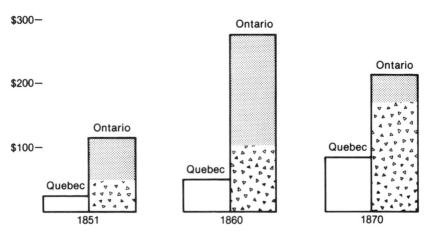

Source: statistical appendix, Table S.5

were affected only by those commodities that were sold outside the agricultural sector. Items that were produced and consumed on the farm were undoubtedly critical to the farmer's well-being, but they did not affect the development of the rest of the economy.

In this vital area of cash income the picture is clear and striking (Figure 4.1). In the early 1850s cash sales of the average Quebec farmer were about one-fifth those of his Ontario counterpart. In the boom years of the mid-1850s this fraction would have fallen to about one-tenth. The proportion was again one-fifth in 1861, which was a year of high wheat exports, and during the 1860s it would have fluctuated between one-fifth and one-third, depending on the state of the wheat trade (see Figure 2.3). By 1871 the wheat staple had entered a permanent decline, and the 40 per cent figure of that year was undoubtedly the highest of the period. In other words, the ratio of the cash income of the average Ontario farmer to that of the Quebec farmer varied between 2.5 to one and 10 to one, and for the period as a whole the ratio would have averaged 4 or 5. That these enormous differences had profound effects on the general development of the two provinces is the central argument of this book. The remainder of this chapter considers the narrower issue as to why the average Quebec farmer's sales of commodities other than wheat were consistently only half those of the Ontario farmer, despite the latter's much greater concentration on wheat production.

Just before mid-century, rising American prices created a market for Canadian produce in that country, and the combined effects of the Reciprocity Treaty,[1] new railway links, and the Civil War ensured that the American market remained important throughout the period. Overseas conditions, it has been seen, affected Canadian agriculture in the 1850s when the Crimean War and European crop failures created an unprecedented demand for North American wheat. In the next decade, conditions in Britain permitted the export of rising quantities of Canadian butter and cheese. At home, railway construction, urban growth, and opportunities for import substitution brought some improvement in the domestic market. These were the major forces facing farmers in both provinces, but a survey of the major markets will demonstrate that the farmers of Ontario responded more effectively than did the farmers of Quebec.

---

1 The Reciprocity Treaty, 1854-66, established free trade in natural products between Canada and the United States. Its effects have been analysed by Arthur Harvey, *The Reciprocity Treaty* (Quebec City, c. 1866); Donald C. Masters, *The Reciprocity Treaty of 1854* (London 1936); L. Officer and L. Smith, 'The Canadian-American Reciprocity Treaty of 1855-1866,' *Journal of Economic History* (1968), 598-623; and Robert E. Ankli, 'The Reciprocity Treaty of 1854,' *Canadian Journal of Economics*, IV, 1 (1971), 1-20.

Figure 4.2
Eximports from Quebec and Ontario, 1850-71

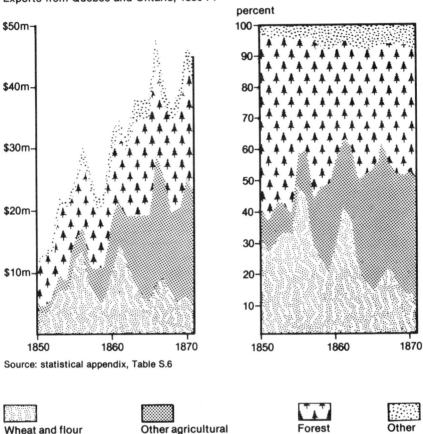

Source: statistical appendix, Table S.6

Wheat and flour   Other agricultural   Forest   Other

    The rise of agricultural exports other than wheat and flour is seen clearly in Figure 4.2. Averaging only $1.7 million per year in the first half of the 1850s, exports in this category rose to an average of $16.8 million in the period 1866-71. Agricultural products other than wheat and flour constituted 9.8 per cent of all Canadian exports in 1850-55 and 39.2 per cent in 1866-71. The major agricultural exports were barley and oats, livestock, and dairy products, and these will be examined in turn.

    Barley became a major export in the 1850s. During the period of free trade with the United States (1854-66), both provinces increased their shipments to that country, although Ontario ports generally accounted for about three-quarters of total Canadian exports.[2] After the abrogation of reciprocity, the superior quality of Ontario barley permitted a continuing growth of exports despite the tariff, but exports from Quebec ports fell rapidly. Exports of oats also rose dramatically, and in this case over two-thirds of the exports were the produce of Quebec. The end of reciprocity brought a gradual decline in the oat trade.

For the Quebec farmer, the trade in coarse grains was the first major source of cash since the decline of wheat, but nevertheless the major share of the benefits went to Ontario. The trade in oats on a large scale lasted no more than ten years, while the barley trade was larger and lasted longer. By 1870, exports of barley and oats from Ontario ports amounted to $4.7 million, compared with $700,000 from Quebec. Barley remained the major crop of much of eastern Ontario and after 1865 of the entire region bordering Lake Ontario until the McKinley tariff of 1890.

Reciprocity also encouraged exports of horses and cattle to the United States, but again the major response came from Ontario. Total exports in this category rose from little more than $1 million before 1862 to a peak just short of $7 million in 1866, the last year of reciprocity. The end of free trade brought a major setback, but by 1871 exports had recovered to $4.3 million. In the earlier years Quebec ports had contributed well over half of the exports in this category, but Quebec's share fell below 50 per cent from 1866 onwards. The French-Canadian horse remained very popular in the United States, but exports had been so large that the breed had deteriorated almost to the point of extinction by the mid-1860s, and many of the horses exported from Quebec in the later part of the period were raised in the Eastern Townships.[3] Evidently, the Ontario farmers responded with more speed and more volume to changing market conditions. This was particularly apparent during the last year of the Reciprocity Treaty when it was advantageous to export as much as possible before the re-imposition of the tariff.

Dairy products also assumed increased importance throughout the period. Exports of butter never exceeded $200,000 before 1856, but they rose to

2 The figures on exports are from the *Trade and Navigation Returns* contained in the appendices to the Journals of the Legislative Assembly. Since the returns give exports of each commodity by port, it has been possible to determine the level of exports from each province. The figures are not useful in determining the share of each province in overseas exports since these were shipped mainly from Quebec. However, the American market was of dominant importance for major commodities other than wheat, butter, and cheese. If anything, the figures overstate exports of Quebec produce, since some Ontario goods were shipped to the United States via Quebec.

3 Robert Leslie Jones, 'The Agricultural Development of Lower Canada, 1850-1867,' *Agricultural History*, XIX (1945), 217-20

over $500,000 by 1859, and, with the opening of the British market, reached $1.3 million in 1865, and $2.9 million in 1871. In most years after 1860 between two-thirds and three-quarters of exports were destined to Britain. Cheese exports were less than $100,000 before 1865 but reached $1.1 million by 1871. The trade figures are of no value in distinguishing between Quebec and Ontario butter and cheese, but in 1871 there were 328 cheese factories in Ontario and only 25 in Quebec.[4] The Eastern Township dairy farmers sent considerable quantities of butter to the United States during the Civil War, but most of the butter for the British market originated in Ontario, especially in the region around Brockville which was noted for the high quality of its butter.[5]

While these were the major categories of exports, other commodities made significant contributions in some years. Wool exports rose to a peak of $1 million under the special market conditions created by the Civil War, and small quantities of sheep were also exported. Generally Ontario accounted for between two-thirds and three-quarters of exports in this category.[6] Exports of meat to Britain began in the late 1860s, but most of these exports consisted of pork, hams, and bacon which were produced largely from hogs imported from Chicago.[7] Exports of peas to Britain were substantial in some years, and, as suggested by production figures and information on receipts at Montreal, most of the peas exported were produced in Ontario.

The home market also became somewhat more attractive to the farmers during this period. In both provinces the farming population declined from about two-thirds of the total in 1850 to between 55 and 60 per cent in 1870. People living in centres with population exceeding a thousand made up 15 per cent of the population in 1850 and 20 per cent in 1870. This shift of population from agriculture to other activities increased the size of the market for those who remained in farming, but the figures suggest only a gradual improvement in this area.

Turning to specific sectors, the railway construction of the 1850s increased local demand for agricultural products, but, as will be demonstrated shortly,

4 M.Q. Innis, 'The Industrial Development of Ontario, 1783-1820,' in J.K. Johnson, ed., *Historical Essays on Upper Canada* (Carleton Library no 82, 1975), 5
5 William J. Patterson, *Statistical Contributions relating to the Trade, Commerce and Navigation of the Dominion of Canada*, second series (Montreal 1875), 90-1; Robert Leslie Jones, *History of Agriculture in Ontario, 1613-1880* (Toronto 1946), 260-3, and 'Agricultural Development of Lower Canada,' 217-18
6 Masters, *The Reciprocity Treaty*, 201, describes the special qualities of Ontario wool which made it desirable in the manufacture of New England worsteds.
7 Jones, *History of Agriculture*, 224

the additional requirements were satisfied largely by imports. The annual direct demand for agricultural products from the forestry sector was in the order of $2 million around 1870.[8] This is a very small figure in comparison with the export values just discussed, especially since the $2 million refers to the end of the period and includes imports. However, the figure excludes any linkage effects of the wood industry, which are considered in a later chapter.

During the wheat and railway boom of the mid-1850s, a large portion of the growth in domestic demand was met by a dramatic rise in imports. Meat imports rose from an average of $100,000 in 1850-53 to $1 million in 1854-57, average cheese imports quadrupled over the same period, and similar jumps occurred for imports of oats, butter, tallow, and lard. In 1857 the *Canadian Merchant's Magazine* wrote: 'Possessing a soil and climate equal, if not superior, to that of the neighbouring states, with no large manufacturing cities of our own to supply, we are yet importers of a large amount of agricultural produce for home consumption. This is particularly the case as regards Western Canada ... It is no wonder that money is scarce in this part of the country, when we import not only our manufactured goods from the other side, but our very beef and mutton, butter, cheese, apples, eggs and vegetables.'[9] In 1860 an Ontario resident wrote: 'We import our beef. Soon we may have to import our wheat.'[10]

In the following decade there was some import substitution in the areas of meat and cheese, although much of the former was produced with American hogs and in some years Chicago mess pork had a virtual monopoly in the Toronto market. Fruit-growing, egg production, and market gardening also developed in response to the growth of the home market during the latter years of this period. While there was some improvement in the home market, farmers continued to depend heavily on export markets.

It is clear that the major share of the benefits from favourable market developments accrued to Ontario farmers. This is most evident in the case of

8 This figure is based on an estimate given in Harold A. Innis and A.R.M. Lower, *Select Documents in Canadian Economic History, 1783-1885* (Toronto 1933), 513 n1, of the demand created by the production of lumber in the Ottawa Valley for the American market in 1870. This production was about 20 per cent of the value of total exports of forest products, and the value of the requirements of this sector was therefore multiplied by five to give the total estimate (an allowance was also made for oats, which were not included in the above source). McCallum, 'Agriculture and Economic Development in Quebec and Ontario to 1870,' unpublished PHD thesis, McGill University, Montreal, 1977, pp. 325-6.
9 Cited in Masters, *The Reciprocity Treaty*, 196-7
10 Cited in Jones, *History of Agriculture*, 210 n59

exports, for which data are relatively plentiful, but there is also evidence that for some commodities Quebec farmers faced competition in their home market from Ontario as well as from the United States.[11] There were several reasons for this situation. Climatic conditions were partially responsible, as in the case of the persistence of Ontario barley exports after 1866.[12] For commodities such as tobacco and fruit also, southern Ontario had a more favourable climate than Quebec.

More important than climate was the availability of capital. In Ontario the shift from wheat to other commodities was a case of successful diversification around the staple product, or the avoidance of the 'staple trap.' It has been seen that Ontario farmers purchased livestock and improved their buildings during the boom years of the mid-1850s, and income from wheat was also very high at the beginning of the 1860s and in 1866-67. The wheat trade provided the farmers with capital to invest in the newer branches of agriculture, while favourable market developments created the incentive to do so. By contrast, the Quebec farmer had no outgoing staple product from which capital funds could be secured. His income from oats was minimal beside the Ontario farmer's revenue from wheat and barley, and he was more than pressed to repay his debts, buy his bread, and establish the next generation on the land. Thus Ontario farmers had vastly superior access to the relatively large amounts of capital needed for the commercial production of cattle, wool, meat, butter, and cheese.

It is well to reflect on the role of luck in economic history. In both provinces it was inevitable that wheat should fall to that continental triumvirate of land shortages, soil exhaustion, and western competition; and the major forces of geography and continental settlement patterns dictated that this should happen in the early nineteenth century in Quebec and in the 1860s in Ontario. Because of a war in Europe and the vagaries of the weather, it happened that in the last years of the Ontario wheat economy the farmers were showered with unprecedented quantities of cash. Because of conditions in the United States, it just happened that this was also a time of profitable investment opportunities in agriculture. By contrast, Quebec farmers received no such windfall in the dying years of their wheat, and even if they had they could have found no major investment outlets under the hopeless

11 For example, Quebec City breweries were supplied with Ontario barley and Montreal buyers purchased cattle in Ontario. Jones, *ibid.*, 210; Hubert LaRue, *Etudes sur les industries du Québec* (Quebec City 1870)

12 An American investigator wrote that the special properties of Ontario barley which permitted the continued growth in exports after 1866 were 'in all probability climatic and due in a measure to the soil.' Jones, *ibid.*, 240

market conditions that confronted Quebec agriculture in the first half of the nineteenth century.

In addition to the objective facts of climate and capital, a third and final reason for the sluggish response of Quebec farmers is to be found in the subjective realm of attitudes and collective psychology. Yet these matters cannot be considered in a vacuum. For two generations or more, the habitant's margin of subsistence had been slender, and objective market circumstances had been unkind. Having just emerged from these conditions, Quebec farmers were found to be slower than their Ontario counterparts in responding to new conditions, although from the middle of the 1870s 'the expansion of dairying in Quebec brought a slowly growing prosperity among the French Canadians and with it a tendency towards better farm management.'[13] In any case, it is impossible to determine how much of the slow response of the 1850s and 1860s reflected a concrete lack of resources and how much was attributable to these more subjective factors. Fortunately, the question is not very important, for both factors are traceable to the agricultural crisis, the causes of which transcended the personal characteristics of Quebec farmers.

13 Jones, 'Agricultural Development of Lower Canada,' 224

5

Urban and commercial development until 1850

Urban development in Quebec and Ontario is a study in contrasts. Between 1850 and 1870 the two largest cities of Quebec made up about three-quarters of the urban population of that province, while the equivalent figure for Ontario was between one-quarter and one-third. To arrive at the share of Quebec's urban population held by Montreal and Quebec City, one would have to include the fifteen largest towns of Ontario in 1850 and the thirty largest towns in 1870. Looking at the matter in a different way, dozens of urban centres filled the Ontario countryside, but outside Montreal and Quebec City the population of Quebec was overwhemingly rural.

It is clear from Table 5.1 that these differences in urban structure had been firmly established by 1850 and that the differences merely intensified in the following two decades. Between 1850 and 1870 the number of towns increased faster in Ontario than in Quebec, and, while the share of Ontario's two largest cities in the urban population actually fell from one-third in 1850 to one-quarter in 1870, Montreal and Quebec City accounted for close to three-quarters of Quebec's urban population throughout the period. The causes of the basic differences in urban structure are therefore to be found in the years before 1850, and this chapter focuses on those years. Urban growth after 1850 cannot be separated from industrial and transportation developments, and these are treated in later chapters.

ONTARIO

Regional patterns of wheat production and urban and industrial development may be seen at a glance in Figures 5.1 to 5.4. In mid-nineteenth-century Ontario there was a striking concentration of activity in the triangle bounded roughly by York County, the Niagara River, and London. The region varies

TABLE 5.1
Population in Quebec and Ontario, 1850-70

1 Number of towns:

	Quebec			Ontario		
	1850	1860	1870	1850	1860	1870
Town size:						
25,000+	2	2	2	1	1	2
5000-25,000	0	1	3	4	8	10
1000-5000	14	18	22	33	50	69
Total	16	21	27	38	59	81

2 Urban and rural population (thousands):

	Quebec			Ontario		
	1850	1860	1870	1850	1860	1870
Town size:						
25,000+	100	141	167	31	45	83
5000-25,000	0	6	20	41	83	95
1000-5000	31	39	42	67	108	149
Total urban	131	187	229	139	236	328
Total rural	759	925	962	813	1160	1293
Total population	890	1112	1192	952	1396	1621
Urban as percentage of total	14.7	16.8	19.2	14.6	16.9	20.2

Source: Census of Canada

somewhat, sometimes extending further east along Lake Ontario and sometimes stopping short of London on the west; but as a snapshot of a rapidly changing scene the general outline is remarkably clear: the areas of highest wheat production tended also to be the areas of greatest urban and industrial development. This was so despite the very recent settlement of the western regions, which, at mid-century, were in the midst of their period of most rapid growth. This pattern suggests that wheat was at the root of urban development, a supposition that will be confirmed by an analysis of the growth of Ontario towns.

Toronto
It was only by virtue of its position as provincial capital that the town of York, with its 'very trifling'[1] trade and its undeveloped hinterland, had

1 This was the phrase of John Howison, *Sketches of Upper Canada* (1821; Toronto 1965), 55.

Figure 5.1

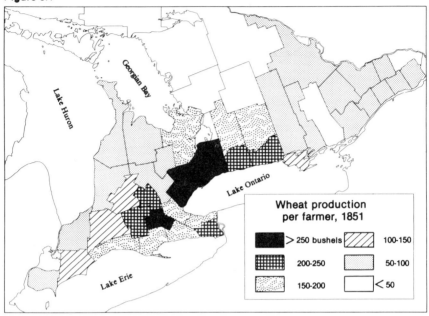

Wheat production per farmer, 1851

- > 250 bushels
- 200-250
- 150-200
- 100-150
- 50-100
- < 50

Figure 5.2

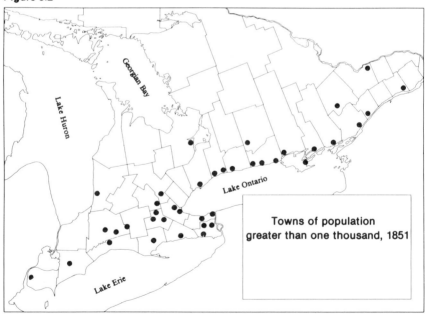

Towns of population greater than one thousand, 1851

Source: Census of Canada

Figure 5.3

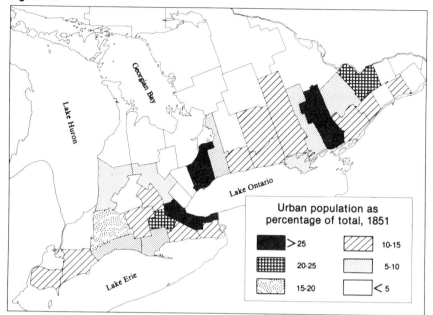

Urban population as percentage of total, 1851

> 25   10-15
20-25   5-10
15-20   < 5

Figure 5.4

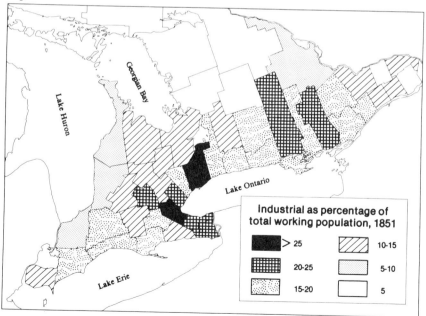

Industrial as percentage of total working population, 1851

> 25   10-15
20-25   5-10
15-20   5

Source: Census of Canada

reached the grand total of 1700 inhabitants by 1824. Starting in the mid-1820s, settlers poured into the Home District, and the district population of 17,000 in 1824 increased at an annual rate of 8.6 per cent to reach 168,000 in 1851. York (or Toronto, as it became in 1834) grew with its agricultural hinterland, attaining a population of 9252 in 1834 and 30,800 in 1851.[2]

The driving force behind the growth of Toronto was the demand for goods and services from the immigrant and farm population. Financed initially by the savings of British immigrants, this demand was maintained by the farmers' cash income from wheat. In the earlier years of settlement, the demand from new arrivals was the major element. In the second half of the 1820s, according to T.W. Acheson, 'the provision of housing, food, clothing, and tools for several hundred new family units each year created a demand which provided the economy with a dynamism otherwise inconceivable.'[3] At the time of the peak immigration of 1831-32, immigrants deposited not less than £300,000 in the Bank of Upper Canada.[4] As exports of wheat and flour accelerated during the 1840s, the demand for goods and services from established farmers was felt with ever-increasing intensity. Throughout the period wheat and flour dominated the export trade of Toronto, accounting for more than three-quarters of exports at mid-century.[5]

As population and trade increased, the importance of the city's position as provincial capital declined correspondingly. Thus, in 1845 W.H. Smith, author of the *Canadian Gazetteer*, wrote: '... the seat of government was moved to Kingston in 1841 ... Had this event taken place ten years sooner, it might have had a serious effect upon the prosperity of the town, but in 1841 Toronto had become a place of too great a commercial importance to feel much ill effect from the removal of the government offices, and the loss of the expenditure of a few thousand pounds per annum.'[6]

2 Population figures for Toronto are from Edith G. Firth, ed., *The Town of York, 1815-1834* (Toronto 1966), xxvi; and Census of Canada, 1870, IV, 83, 131, 178. Unless otherwise stated, figures on town population are from the census.

3 Acheson, 'The Nature and Structure of York Commerce in the 1820's' (1969), in J.K. Johnson, ed., *Historical Essays on Upper Canada* (Carleton Library no 82, 1975), 171

4 Jacob Spelt, *Urban Development in South-Central Ontario* (Carleton Library no 57, 1972), 79

5 Unless otherwise stated, information on export and import values is from I.D. Andrews, *Report on the Trade, Commerce, and Resources of the British North American Colonies ...* 31st Congress, 2nd Session, ex. doc. no 23 (Washington 1851), and Andrews, *Report on the Trade and Commerce of the British North American Colonies and upon the Trade of the Great Lakes and Rivers*, 32nd Congress, 1st Session, ex. doc. no 136 (Washington 1853).

6 Smith cited in Spelt, *Urban Development*, 94

Under these circumstances the primary functions of Toronto were to export flour and to import goods for sale to established and prospective farmers. Acheson described the operations of the retailers around 1830. About 90 per cent of the market of Toronto's retailers was in rural areas, and consequently the pattern of sales was determined by the farming seasons. Peak sales occurred in October following the harvest, and business remained fairly strong throughout most of the winter when the farmers transported their wheat and flour to the town. Demand fell off during the spring thaw, and it picked up again in July when there was a steady demand for tools and implements. The 'struggling' patrons purchased cotton cloth and thread, glass, nails, scythes, and hardware supplies, while the more prosperous customers bought luxury articles such as Madeira, snuff, and silk. These prosperous customers, presumably mainly attached to government activities, were small in number, and it was the agricultural population which determined both the seasonal fluctuations and the principal commodity composition of retail sales.

Behind the retailers were the wholesalers. These were larger commercial enterprises which not only sold goods to the retailers but also purchased and exported flour. As will be demonstrated in Chapter 7, manufacturing made modest progress in the years to 1850, and the goods supplied by the wholesalers were mainly imported. In the early years most imports were British goods purchased through Montreal, but after the opening of the Erie Canal in 1825 the wholesalers began to import more American goods. In the prosperous years of the late 1820s and early 1830s, larger and more specialized wholesalers established themselves, and to stay in business it became necessary to import goods directly from Britain.[7] In 1832 York had eight wholesalers; by 1850 this number had increased to twenty, fifteen of which had jettisoned retail activities altogether.[8]

Indeed, by mid-century a rising commercial group led by the wholesalers was challenging the position held by the old Toronto families. This group had arrived in the 1830s, and included such men as William McMaster (wholesaler and later banker) and F.C. Capreol (commercial salesroom operator and later railway promoter). Many of the old members of the Family Compact were still important in the economic life of the city, but by 1850 they were losing power to the newer group led by the wholesalers.[9]

7 Firth, *Town of York*, xxvi-viii
8 Barry D. Dyster, 'Toronto, 1840-1860: Making It in a British Protestant Town,' unpublished PHD thesis, University of Toronto, 1970; and Firth, *ibid.*, 75-6
9 Donald C. Masters, *The Rise of Toronto*, 1850-1890 (Toronto 1947), 21-6; and Dyster, *ibid.*, 293

While this commercial development based on settlement and wheat exports applied on a smaller scale to most other Ontario towns, a number of special factors favoured Toronto over other places. Between 1824 and 1829 York had the only bank in the province, but in the latter year the Bank of Montreal established a branch in York, and banks were established in Hamilton and Kingston in the first half of the 1830s. While the Bank of Upper Canada was sometimes credited with York's growing prosperity, it was remarked in 1831 that 'the fine back Country does infinitely more for the advancement of York than the Bank can do.'[10] To the advantages of an early lead in banking and an exceptionally large and fertile back country were added a good harbour, an early road, and the town's position as provincial capital, which made it a focal point for new arrivals to the province. It was only natural, then, that Toronto should be the main beneficiary of any trends in the direction of increased geographical concentration of economic activity.

In the years to 1850, such forces of concentration were limited. Toronto's export trade was not markedly higher than that of other lake ports, and according to Jacob Spelt its presence did not have any influence on the size or number of manufacturing establishments in York County. The one important sector of the economy in which forces of concentration had begun to assert themselves by mid-century was wholesale trade. In 1851 the value of direct imports to Toronto was $2.6 million, as compared with $2.2 million for Hamilton and $1 million for Kingston. The next largest importer was Chippewa at $318,000. By 1850 Toronto had established itself as the major distributing point for such ports as Oakville, Port Credit, and Whitby. There were economies to be gained in limiting the number of contacts with British and American suppliers, and 'it was only natural that this trade should concentrate on the capital, the largest city and market with the biggest banks and one of the best ports.'[11]

Furthermore, Toronto had started to invade the territory formerly held by Montreal. The city's direct imports (as opposed to goods imported through Montreal wholesalers) rose dramatically in the 1840s and imports from the United States more than doubled in the two years between 1849 and 1851. It has been seen that Toronto wholesalers began to import goods directly from the early 1830s, and in the same period they started to replace Montrealers as suppliers to merchants in smaller Ontario towns. Also, from the late 1840s a rising proportion of wheat and flour was shipped through the United States instead of through Montreal.

10 John Macauly, agent of the bank at Kingston, cited in Firth, *Town of York,*, xxxi
11 Spelt, *Urban Development*, 75-6, 79

Toronto's development is therefore explained not only by the growth of its own hinterland but also by a start to its commercial penetration of other regions. In the process it began its escape from the control of Montreal. On the whole, however, the city's growth up to 1850 depended mainly on growth within its own territory, for, with the partial exception of wholesale trade, dispersion rather than concentration remained the hallmark of economic activity.

Finally, associated with all this was the accumulation of capital. Funds were derived first from the savings of immigrants and from the disposal of land held by the government and its associates, and then increasingly from the activities of the rising merchant class and its agricultural hinterland. Local governments, deriving their revenue directly from the wealth of the towns and countryside, were also important contributors. The uses to which the funds were put are analysed in later chapters, but the point to be emphasized at present is that all these sources may be traced to the twin processes of settlement and wheat exports.

Hamilton

Hamilton owed its early growth to its position at the head of Lake Ontaio. According to W.H. Smith, 'Hamilton is admirably suited for carrying on a large wholesale trade with the West, – being at the head of navigation of Lake Ontario, and in the heart of the best settled portion of the Province, it possesses peculiar advantages for receiving goods, and distributing them through the interior, while its central position makes it the depôt of a large extent of grain and other produce.'[12] The town's population reflected the course of settlement and the wheat trade. The Burlington Bay Canal, which connected Hamilton with Lake Ontario, was completed in 1825, and in 1831 it was said that 'since the Burlington Canal started, Hamilton has increased from 3 to 18 stores. Its former trifling trade and its houses have doubled.' Population rose from 1400 in 1833 to 3600 in 1837, 4300 in 1842, and 14,000 in 1851.[13]

As in the case of Toronto, this growth resulted from the rapid settlement of the city's back country and the acceleration of wheat exports during the 1840s. The population of the Gore District was 150,000 in 1851, or more than six times as high as in 1831. Exports of wheat and flour more than tripled between 1838 and 1844, and they had tripled again by 1850. By mid-

12 Smith, *Canada: Past, Present and Future*, 2 vols. (Toronto 1851), I, 223
13 *Western Mercury*, cited in Marjorie Freeman Campbell, *A Mountain and a City: The Story of Hamilton* (Toronto 1966), 65; population statistics, *ibid.*, 62

century, Hamilton exported more wheat and flour than any Ontario town except Port Dalhousie, located at the mouth of the Welland Canal.

As Smith indicated, Hamilton was the major wholesale centre for points west of Lake Ontario. Douglas McCalla has produced a map that reveals, for the year 1857, the deep penetration into western Ontario by Hamilton's largest wholesaler, Buchanan, Harris and Company. Eighty centres from Niagara to Amherstburgh and from Lake Erie to points north of Goderich contained one or more customers of this firm, and the most concentrated group of customers was located between London and Hamilton.[14]

Hamilton, then, was a commercial town. In his exhaustive study of the town in 1851 Michael B. Katz wrote that '... men in commerce, about a quarter of the workforce, controlled nearly 59% of the wealth, a figure which underscores the clear commercial basis of the city.' As in Toronto, the industrial sector, operating overwhelmingly in local markets, played a passive role in the years up to 1850. The settlement and development of Hamilton's rich and rapidly growing agricultural hinterland was the basis not only of the town's growth but also of the wealth and capital accumulation of the commercial class. The export of wheat and flour, the importation and distribution of manufactured goods, land speculation, and personal profit derived from municipal funds[15] were all based directly or indirectly on the settler's supply of wheat and demand for land and other goods and services. This capital accumulation and general prosperity may be seen in a number of developments: the replacement of wooden structures with brick buildings and the 'vast improvement' in the character of the city's buildings in the last few years of the 1840s, the location of two bank headquarters and four branches in Hamilton, improvements such as the introduction of gas lighting in 1851, and the ambitious but misguided decision of the city to subscribe £100,000 for the construction of the Great Western Railway.[16]

This is not to paint a picture of general affluence and social harmony. As Katz demonstrated minutely, inequalities were enormous and individual business failures were commonplace. The large-scale Irish immigration brought problems of disease, riots and violence. Nevertheless, during the last decade of the pre-railway age, Hamilton underwent a total transformation in its population, trade, social infrastructure, and wealth. It is impossible

14 McCalla, 'The Decline of Hamilton as a Wholesale Center,' *Ontario History*, LXV (1973), 253
15 Katz, 'The People of a Canadian City: 1851-2,' *Canadian Historical Review*, LIII, (1972), 411. Katz, in *The People of Hamilton, Canada West* (Cambridge, Mass. 1975), provides evidence that these were the primary sources of income of the 'entrepreneurial' class.
16 Smith, *Canada*, I, 220-8; Campbell, *A Mountain and a City*, 76

to attribute this transformation to anything other than agricultural settlement and the growth of wheat and flour exports.

Other Ontario towns
The maps in Figures 5.1 to 5.4 indicate that the three westernmost counties of Ontario were not large-scale wheat producers and that they were relatively underdeveloped in terms of both urban and industrial growth. The only two towns of a thousand or more were Amherstburg (1880) and Chatham (2070). The former was a frontier post and naval depot during the War of 1812, and it continued to be a garrison town until after 1850. In 1850 and 1851 almost all enumerated exports consisted of wheat, but the quantities involved were not large. By Ontario standards Amherstburg was stagnant. Joseph Bouchette in 1831 gave the population as over 1200 and mentioned 'the wealth and respectability of its inhabitants.'[17] In the twenty years to 1851 population rose by only 50 per cent. The difficulties of wheat growing in the region and the correspondingly low production levels would seem to have limited the growth of the town. Chatham, on the other hand, was a product of the wheat boom. Its population rose from 812 in 1841 to 2070 in 1851, and, according to Smith, 'Being situated in the midst of a fine agricultural country, it is a place of considerable business.' Or in the words of F.C. Hamil, 'The principal source of prosperity for the town was the prolific country about it, settled by industrious, intelligent, and thrifty farmers.'[18] During the 1840s property values rose rapidly, bank branches were established, and brick houses began to replace less solid structures. In 1850 the town had two steam grist mills, two steam sawmills, two foundries and machine shops, a brewery, two tanneries, a woollen factory, and four distilleries.[19]. Nevertheless, taken as a whole, the three counties of the Western District grew relatively little wheat, and difficulties in this area had led to an effort to expand tobacco production and in general to adopt a more diversified agriculture. Tobacco and other products were not good substitutes for large quantities of wheat, and the overall development of the district was meagre.

Moving eastwards, London, St Thomas, and Ingersoll were within about thirty miles of each other in Middlesex, Oxford, and Elgin counties. The maps indicate that in 1850 this area was more developed than the counties to

17 Bouchette, *The British Dominions in North America ... and a Topographical Dictionary of Lower Canada*, 2 vols. (1831; New York 1968), I, 105-6
18 Smith, *Canada*, I, 16; Fred Coyne Hamil, *The Valley of the Lower Thames, 1640 to 1850* (Toronto 1951), 263
19 Unless otherwise stated, information on the industrial and commercial establishments of each town in 1850 is from Smith, *Canada*.

the west and somewhat less developed than the counties along the shores of Lake Ontario. This was a newer region which at mid-century was in the middle of its period of most rapid growth: the population of the London District tripled during the 1840s, while the town of London grew from 1100 in 1834 to 2600 in 1842 and 7000 in 1851.[20] London became the district town in 1826, and in 1838 an imperial garrison was stationed in the town. These factors were the major non-agricultural influences on London's development, and, while they may explain the town's ascendancy over St Thomas, they were relatively unimportant in the urban development of the region as a whole. Some town in the region had to be the district centre, and, while the coming of the garrison in 1837 was a shot in the arm for the town's economy, its departure in 1853 was 'almost unnoticed.'[21]

After London was given the right to hold a public market in 1835, it quickly became the trade focus of a rich but very partially settled agricultural area. It was during the 1840s that London's economy became firmly based on wheat. In the words of Orlo Miller: 'By the late 1840's, London's economy had become tied to a more stable commodity than either litigation or logistics [that is, district centre or garrison town]. That commodity was wheat ... By the middle of the nineteenth century Western Ontario had become one vast granary and London one of its principal market towns and shipping centres.'[22]

As London grew, it attracted men with capital to invest and enriched those who were already there. Some of the town's leading citizens arrived with the settlers in the 1820s and early 1830s. This group included George Goodhue, merchant and land speculator, and Ellis Hyman and Simeon Morrill, both tanners. Men such as Elijah Leonard, iron founder and steam engine maker; John Birrell, dry goods wholesaler; and Thomas Carling, brewer, arrived soon after the Rebellion of 1837. John K. Labatt, brewer; Charles Hunt, miller; and the McClary brothers, warehousing, arrived in the late 1840s and early 1850s. These manufacturers and wholesalers served an area that 'stretched west to Chatham, Windsor, and Sarnia, north to Goderich, St Mary's, and Stratford, east to Ingersoll and Woodstock, and south to St Thomas and Port Stanley.' Strong commercial ties with Hamilton were deve-

20 The population figure for 1834 is from Frederick H. Armstrong and Daniel J. Brock, 'The Rise of London: A Study of Urban Evolution in Nineteenth-Century Southwestern Ontario,' in Armstrong et al., eds., Aspects of Nineteenth-Century Ontario (Toronto 1974), 89.
21 Orlo Miller, 'The Fat Years, and the Lean: London (Canada) in Boom and Depression,' Ontario History, LIII (1961), 76
22 Ibid., 74

loped from an early date. By 1850 London had four bank branches, two building societies, several insurance companies, three 'extensive' foundries, one grist and sawmill, three breweries, two distilleries, two tanneries, and three newspapers. While provincial funds were spent generously on London roads because the position of public works commissioner was held by a London citizen, it was the local capital of such families as the Labatts and Carlings which paid for the road to the Huron Tract in 1849 and for the London–Port Stanley railroad in the 1840s.[23]

Ingersoll, Woodstock, and St Thomas were rivals of London in the 1820s and 1830s, but by 1850 they were clearly of secondary importance. To some extent they suffered from London's success, as in the case of Elijah Leonard's departure from St Thomas to London in 1838 on the conviction that London was 'sooner or later to become the hub of Western Canada.'[24] Nevertheless, the populations of Ingersoll and Woodstock grew extremely rapidly in the late 1840s, and it was not until the railway age that these towns suffered severely from the forces of concentration. At mid-century they were market centres surrounded by a booming agriculture, and each had its five to ten mills and manufactories. The same was true on a lesser scale for the fifteen to twenty smaller villages which dotted the countryside within a twenty-mile radius of London.

Goderich served as district town headquarters of the Canada Company and port for the surrounding country. Population rose from 300 in 1831[25] to about 1300 in 1851, and in the latter year the town had the usual assortment of mills, newspapers, and bank and insurance company agents. Exports were still very low, and the most important function in 1850 was to supply settlers bound for the northern sections of the Huron Tract.

In Norfolk County only the district town of Simcoe had as many as one thousand people. Lumber was more important in this county than elsewhere, and in 1850 Ports Dover, Ryerse, and Rowan exported mainly wood, although in the first of these, which was much the largest, wheat and flour made up close to half the total value of exports. None of these ports contained as many as a thousand residents. Simcoe, which had the usual quota of mills and other establishments, derived its existence from a combination of wood, wheat, and administrative functions.

We come now to the largest cluster of towns, those within about forty miles of Hamilton in Brant and Wentworth counties and in the Niagara

23 Armstrong and Brock, 'Rise of London,' 83-4, 91; Miller, *Ibid.*, 76
24 Cited in Armstrong and Brock, 'Rise of London,' 91
25 Bouchette, *British Dominions*, I, 118

Peninsula. A glance at Figure 5.1 shows that this region was second only to the neighbourhood of Toronto in its wheat production. In Brant County wheat production per farmer was the highest in the province in 1851 (370 bushels), and this county contained Paris and Brantford, with a combined population of 5800 or 23 per cent of total county population. Brantford, the largest of these towns, increased its population rapidly in the few years before 1850. It had the advantage of being located on the Grand River and on the Hamilton-London road. In 1850, 350,000 bushels of wheat and flour (just under three-quarters of the total value of shipments) were shipped from Brantford along the Grand River, and in addition 'large quantities of flour, whisky and ashes are teamed down to Hamilton and shipped there.' The manufacturing establishments seem to have been larger than average, for Smith lists 'four grist mills, one of which is a large brick building; two foundries, doing a large business; a stone-ware manufactory, the only one yet in operation in the west of Canada ... two tanneries, two breweries, four distilleries, a planing machine and a sash factory, &c. &c.'[26]

The other towns on the Grand River had similar, if somewhat lesser, manufacturing activities, and they too profited from their position on the river in the midst of highly productive wheat farming. Galt and Guelph had originated as supply centres for the Canada Company, but by mid-century most of the lands in the region had been settled. Dunnville was located at the mouth of the Grand River and was a point of trans-shipment of imports as well as an export point. In 1850 wheat and flour made up about three-quarters of the town's exports.

In the Niagara District the largest town, St Catharines, benefited from its position on the Welland Canal and had six grist mills. Thorold was also on the Welland Canal, and it had grown rapidly in the few years prior to 1850, taking advantage of the hydraulic powers of the canal to establish a number of large grist mills and other enterprises. Niagara and Chippewa had declined somewhat with the opening of the Welland Canal: in 1851 they had a combined population of about 4500.

The Lake Ontario wheat ports east of Hamilton and west of Belleville were so similar that they may be described as a group. According to figures contained in Smith, for six of the eight ports in this region wheat and flour accounted for at least 80 per cent of total exports. The two exceptions were Port Hope and Cobourg, but these were also the only two towns (except Toronto) for which figures on exports to places other than the United States were not available. Most of the towns had wheat and flour exports between

26 Smith, *Canada*, I, 237-9

175,000 and 300,000 bushels and total exports of $160,000 to $320,000, while the value of imports varied more widely. The ports competed for their respective back countries, and leading citizens were active in promoting and financing roads, and later railroads, to tap their agricultural hinterlands. Financial services and small-scale manufacturing of the type already described had developed in all of these towns by 1850.

This survey of towns in the wheat-producing areas of Ontario ends with Barrie and Peterborough, which were inland towns north of Lake Ontario. Barrie, with a population of 1007 in 1851, was the main supply centre for the settlers and farmers of Simcoe County, as well as the county town. Its growth had been moderate, and it contained a tannery, brewery, newspaper, and bank agency in 1850. Peterborough was more substantial, with a population of 2191 in 1851. Immigration and the settlement of the surrounding districts remained the town's most important function until about 1840, after which the export of wheat, flour, and lumber increased in importance. In 1850 wheat and flour exports were of about the same importance as exports of lumber and square timber.[27]

We come now to the towns in the part of the province which did not produce wheat as a staple product. From Hastings County eastwards there were in 1851 nine towns with population exceeding one thousand, of which the largest were Kingston (11,600), Bytown (7800), Belleville (4600), and Brockville (2200). For the region as a whole, the urban population made up 15.1 per cent of the total. This was a lower proportion then in the former districts of Niagara (19.1 per cent), Home (21 per cent), and Gore (18 per cent), but it was higher than in most counties west of Brant. Considering that this eastern section had been settled earliest, its urban development up to 1850 was not impressive.

In 1830 Kingston had a larger population than York and about four times as many people as Hamilton; by 1851 it had been surpassed by Hamilton and had less than 40 per cent of the population of Toronto. The economy of Kingston had traditionally been based on its position as entrepôt, together with civilian and military government establishments, the lumber trade through the Rideau Canal, and shipbuilding. The town's unproductive back country was said to have restrained its growth, and it suffered setbacks with the movement of the capital to Montreal in 1844 and the decline of its role as entrepôt. Smith wrote that 'the Goverment establish-

27 Thomas W. Poole, *A Sketch of the Early Settlement and Subsequent Progress of the Town of Peterborough* (Peterborough 1867), 93-9. Estimate of price of square timber is from Smith, *Canada*, II, 229.

ments, naval and military, with the shipping interest, are the principal support of the city.'[28]

Bytown (later Ottawa) was clearly a lumber town, and Belleville exported mainly wood in 1850, although wheat and flour were significant (28 per cent of exports). To a large extent, Prescott and Brockville were dependent on St Lawrence shipping, while Perth was originally the supply centre for local settlers and in later years had been connected to the Rideau Canal by a private company. Cornwall lost population between 1845 and 1850, and the small towns of Napanee and Picton were market centres. Of the nine towns, only Belleville, Kingston, and Bytown had significant exports in 1850. Taken as a whole, the region from Belleville eastwards experienced slightly more than a doubling of its urban population between 1835 and 1850. West of Belleville, urban population rose by a factor of five over the same period.[29]

This analysis has covered the years up to 1850. In the next twenty years the number of towns increased from 38 to 81. Three-quarters of the newly established towns were located west of Trenton, and most of these were in the more recently settled inland countries which accounted for a rising proportion of wheat production as the older lands became exhausted. Dispersion remained the keynote of urban structure, as the share of the five largest cities in the urban population actually fell from 51 per cent in 1850 to 40 per cent in 1870.

Three sets of conclusions flow from this analysis. First, wheat was the driving force behind at least twenty-six of the twenty-nine towns west of Belleville (Amherstburg, Simcoe, and Peterborough were partial exceptions). All of these towns were either export ports or inland transportation terminals for Ontario wheat, all were market centres for the agricultural population, most had been supply centres for settlers, and many were import ports or wholesale centres. Wood and garrisons had been of secondary or passing importance. In addition to the centres of over a thousand people, there were literally hundreds of lesser centres, concentrated in the most productive wheat-producing areas, which performed similar functions on a smaller scale. By producing the region's only major export and by providing the market for its imports, agriculture was the foundation of commercial activity. Also, it was this wheat-generated activity that attracted men of capital to the region's commercial and nascent industrial sectors, that provided

28 Smith, *Canada*, II, 278. Direct imports by Kingston were 74 per cent of direct imports of all Ontario ports in 1842. This ratio declined to an average of 30 per cent in 1844-46 and 10 per cent in 1848-51. Andrews, *Report on the Trade, Commerce, and Resources*, 198-9; *Report on the Trade and Commerce*, 457-8.

29 Estimates of urban population in 1835 are from Albert Faucher, *Québec en Amérique au XIXe siècle* (Montreal 1973), 301.

the basis for further capital accumulation, and that provided the tax base and savings that financed the roads and other projects of the time.

Furthermore, by the standards of the day the wheat economy of 1850 was an economic success story. In the words of I.D. Andrews, the compiler of the most comprehensive statistics on the trade of the province, 'The population of Toronto has doubled in the last 10 years, and is now 30,000. Hamilton, now containing 14,000, has been equally progressive. The imports show their commercial program to have been equally rapid; and there can be little doubt that in Upper Canada the export of produce, and the import and consumption of all the substantial and necessary products of civilization, are as high, per head, as in the best agricultural districts of the United States.'[30]

The second conclusion is that wood had much weaker effects on urban growth than wheat. The eastern part of the province had been settled earlier, and the Ottawa Valley was the major contributor to Canada's very large exports of forest products (Figure 3.2). Yet urban growth in this region had been meagre. The reasons for this are discussed in a later chapter.

The final conclusion concerns the pattern of urban growth. Why was this growth so dispersed instead of highly concentrated in a single city, as in the case of Winnipeg in the prairie wheat economy? Why, indeed, was the commercial activity located in Ontario at all, when, for example, most of the commercial activity associated with southern cotton and much of that flowing from prairie wheat took place outside the staple-producing region? To these questions, so vital to the prospects of any staple-producing region, there are two basic answers. The technology of the mid-nineteenth century favoured dispersion. We have already mentioned the case of the tiny port of Oakville which transported the wheat to its warehouses, constructed the steam engines and flour mill machinery that converted the wheat to flour, and built and manned the ships that carried the finished commodity to Montreal.[31] In 1847 a small Peterborough foundry manufactured most of the threshing mills used in the district, as well as a wide variety of the agricultural implements.[32] Such examples could be multiplied, but, in general, technology in the areas of transportation and manufacturing favoured the very local retention of a very high proportion of the linkages flowing from the wheat staple.

This technological bias in favour of the local level naturally promoted the retention of commercial activity within the province. However, even in 1850

30 Andrews, *Report on the Trade and Commerce*, 430.
31 Hazel C. Mathews, *Oakville and the Sixteen: The History of an Ontario Port* (Toronto 1953), 204, 212
32 Poole, *Sketch of the Early Settlement*, 62

technology favoured a higher degree of concentration of imports and whole-salers, and in subsequent years technological changes promoted centraliza-tion of other activities. The question was whether these centralized activities would take place in Ontario or Quebec, and it was the availability of direct American imports and the American trade route that tipped the balance in favour of Ontario. By contrast, fifty years later the prairie wheat economy had no such escape from eastern control, for the high Canadian tariffs and the monopolistic American freight rates made it difficult to import goods or export wheat through the United States.[33] In the case of Ontario, the effec-tive challenge to Montreal's monopoly position had permitted a growing in-dependence on the part of Toronto wholesalers from the 1830s, and the story was to be repeated in banking, transportation, and industry. Neverthe-less, this was a gradual and partial process, for it will be seen in the next section that Montreal derived much benefit from the Ontario wheat economy.

QUEBEC

Montreal
Much, if not most, of the literature on this period has concerned itself with the commercial empire of the St Lawrence, and there is no need to repeat the story of the Montreal merchants here.[34] Suffice it to say that a series of shocks in the 1840s destroyed both the old colonial system and Montreal's aspirations for the trade of the American west. Abandoned by Britain and excluded from American produce and markets, the Montreal merchants were driven to the Annexation Manifesto of 1849, in which they declared that the only solution to their problems lay in 'going to prosperity, since prosperity will not come to us.'[35]

Excluding for the moment its role as supplier of cheap labour, Quebec agriculture had little to do with the development of Montreal. The local farmers had made no significant contribution to exports since the early years

33 In comparison with mid-century Ontario, the prairies also faced more highly developed manufacturing and financial centres to the east, as well as a transportation network which denied to its nascent industry the 'natural protection' enjoyed by Ontario in its early years of industrial growth. The comparison with the prairies is analysed further in Chapter 8.
34 Works in this area include D.G. Creighton, *The Commercial Empire of the St. Lawrence, 1760-1850* (Toronto 1937); Gilbert N. Tucker, *The Canadian Commercial Revolution, 1845-1851* (New Haven 1936); and R.T. Naylor, 'The Rise and Fall of the Third Com-mercial Empire of the St Lawrence' in Gary Teeple, ed., *Capitalism and the National Question in Canada* (Toronto 1972).
35 Cited in Tucker, *Canadian Commercial Revolution*, 186.

of the century, their demand for imports was limited by their low and fluctuating incomes, and their role in capital formation was minimal. They supplied a portion of the city's livestock requirements, little of its wheat, and most of its limited requirements for other vegetable products.

On the other hand, Ontario agriculture was a major factor in the economy of Montreal. While Montreal never became the great emporium of the American mid-west, such shipments as it did receive came increasingly from Ontario rather than from the United States. Thus, wheat and flour shipments via the St Lawrence rose from 2.9 million bushels in 1840 to a peak of 5.8 million bushels in 1847, and by 1851 shipments were 4.3 million bushels. Ontario produce was less than half the total in 1840 and virtually all of it in 1850. In the latter year, wheat and flour made up 78 per cent of the total tonnage passing down the St Lawrence canals. This excludes lumber products which accounted for 10 per cent of the tolls collected.[36] Thus, by 1850 Ontario wheat and flour were of dominant importance in the shipments received at Montreal via the St Lawrence canals. The total tonnage, while not as great as had been anticipated, would have been almost negligible without the wheat and flour of the upper province.[37]

Montreal's imports were closely tied to conditions in Ontario. According to Fernand Ouellet, even by 1820 the incomes of Montreal importers were 'directement fonction de l'agriculture haut-canadienne.'[38] As indicated by the following figures, the volume of merchandise passing up the Lachine Canal to Ontario rose dramatically:[39]

36 Andrews, *Report on the Trade, Commerce, and Resources*, 276-7
37 As noted above, the exclusion of shipments to Lower Canada and the Maritimes gives a false impression of the relative importance of the American route. This misleading impression is compounded by considering only wheat, in which case, according to Easterbrook and Aitken, as cited in Jean Hamelin and Yves Roby, *Histoire économique du Québec, 1851-1896* (Montreal 1971), 47-8, the volume of Upper Canadian wheat exported by the American route was more than fifteen times that exported via the St Lawrence in 1850. The more meaningful figure, as given in Table S.2, includes flour shipments as well as shipments destined to Lower Canada and the Maritimes, and on this basis St Lawrence shipments were one-third greater than those via the United States in 1850 and 88 per cent greater in 1851.
38 Ouellet, *Histoire économique et sociale du Québec, 1760-1850* (Montreal 1971), 265
39 1826: *Journals of the Legislative Assembly of Lower Canada* (JLALC), 1830, app. D
1830: JLALC, 1831, app. G
1835: JLALC, 1835-36, app. Q
1844: *Journals of the Legislative Assembly of Canada* (JLAC), 1844-45, app. AA
1850: Andrews, *Report on the Trade, Commerce, and Resources*, 282-3
All figures refer to the Lachine Canal except in the year 1850, which refers to the St Lawrence canals. However, these would seem to be almost identical, since in 1844 shipments were 26,600 tons via the St Lawrence canals and 27,500 tons via the Lachine Canal.

1826	1500 tons
1830	8300 tons
1835	15,800 tons
1844	27,500 tons
1850	70,000 tons

In 1851 *direct* imports to Ontario towns via Montreal amounted to $3.0 million, as compared with $9.2 million entered as imports at Montreal.[40] A significant but unknown percentage of the latter figure would have been re-exported to Ontario.

Thus Ontario provided the great majority of Montreal's exports and absorbed perhaps one-half of the imports which reached the city. For Montreal, the upper province was the one bright sport in an otherwise gloomy decade. This is all the more remarkable in the light of Ontario's shift to the American route for both its imports and exports: the province's growth was so rapid that Montreal's declining share of the trade did not prevent the city's absolute level from growing at impressive rates.

For reasons discussed in a later chapter, there was little progress in manufacturing during the 1840s, and this, together with the commercial disappointments of the decade, led to the emigration of large numbers of workers. Referring to 'Montreal and Quebec workmen' as the first class of emigrants, a Select Committee of the Legislative Assembly in 1849[41] described the causes of this emigration in the following terms:

– unsettled trade and industry for several years past
– want of manufactories for those previously in lumbering
– increase in U.S. wages and fall here
– lack of public works

It was not until the industrial growth of the 1850s and 1860s that Montreal began to call on the surplus labour of rural Quebec.

Other Quebec towns
The timber trade and shipbuilding dominated the economic life of Quebec City. Local agriculture was of minor importance. Neither did Ontario agriculture exert much influence on Quebec, for while the city was a major exporter of wheat this trade was much less important than the trade in timber and ships.

40 Andrews, *Report on the Trade and Commerce*, 454-5, 458
41 JLAC, 1849, app. AAAAA, 3

In the rest of the province the major activity was agriculture, and Quebec agriculture was a miserable base for urban growth. Worse than this, the crisis in Quebec agriculture destroyed the economic base of established merchants and artisans, and rural artisans who were 'réduits à la misère par l'effondrement du revenu de leurs clients' were forced to emigrate. The Select Committee of 1849 ascribed the emigration of 'workmen who had settled in the villages and county parts' to the fact that the farmers 'do themselves almost everything they might require from a tradesman,' with the result that 'the workmen ... have little employment and lose courage.' Also, the inability of the habitants to repay debt to 'the fearful number of those who carry on trade in our country parts on a small scale' brought financial ruin to debtor and creditor alike.[42]

Outside Montreal and Quebec City the urban population made up 4 per cent of the total population in 1850 and 6 per cent in 1870. Even these figures understate the differential impact of agriculture in the two provinces. While the great majority of Ontario towns owed their existence to the wheat economy, most Quebec towns depended in large measure on activities other than agriculture. This has already been demonstrated for Montreal and Quebec City, and it was also the case for most of the remaining fourteen towns of mid-nineteenth-century Quebec.

The growth of Lachine was obviously not dependent on agricultural conditions, while Aylmer was an Ottawa Valley lumbering town. The economy of St Jean was based on its role as entrepôt for trade between Canada and the United States. Trois-Rivières was in the midst of a region of very poor soil and an agricultural back country which had little to buy or sell. Growth was based on the town's position as a half-way point between Quebec and Montreal, a minor administrative centre, and, from 1840, the exporter of wood from the country along the St Maurice. Laprairie was a commercial centre at the head of communication from Montreal to St Jean and the Richelieu, while Ste Thérèse was a lumbering centre.[43]

In Quebec the railway age began slightly before 1850. The Longueuil–St Hyacinthe section of the St Lawrence and Atlantic Railway was completed in 1847, and these towns had become distribution points based on the railway.[44] Sherbrooke, which had 350 people in 1830, had 2998 in 1851, thanks in large part to the local railroad construction going on at the time of the census. Without the railroad, Sherbrooke 'n'aurait jamais dépassé la taille d'un

42 Ouellet, *Histoire économique et sociale*, 475; JLAC, ibid., 3,11
43 Raoul Blanchard, *Le centre du Canada français* (Montreal 1947), 153-6, 159-62, 166-8;
   L'ouest du Canada français (Montreal 1953), 139, 145
44 Hamelin and Roby, *Histoire économique*, 122-3, 125

Lennoxville ou d'un Richmond.'[45] Joliette, or Industrie as it was called before 1864, originated as a sawmill site in 1823. Under the energetic direction of its founder, the site acquired a flour mill in 1824, a wool factory and nail factory in 1825, a distillery in 1840, and a foundry in 1844. In 1850 a railway was constructed at a cost of $55,000, and at that time population doubled to about 2500. The towns of L'Assomption and Berthier were the two terminal points of this railway.[46]

Sorel and Berthier had been important centres of the wheat trade in earlier years, and the timber trade and shipbuilding were also important in the former. Population of both towns slightly more than doubled in the twenty years to 1850.[47] Finally, Montmagny, which with the exception of Quebec was the only town east of Trois-Rivières with as many as a thousand people, was dependent on local agriculture. Small manufacturing enterprises were encouraged by water power, local raw materials, river transport, and 'l'emploi de l'abondante main-d'œuvre d'origine agricole.'[48] Thus, Quebec towns were only partly based on agriculture. The wood industry and entrepôt and administrative functions were also important, and in some cases railways provided stimuli unrelated to local agriculture.

Consequently, the agricultural sector of mid-nineteenth-century Quebec sustained less than 20,000 town-dwellers. By contrast, the great majority of Ontario's 130,000 urban residents owed their livelihood to economic activity spawned by the wheat staple, and even Montreal, after its grander designs had been shattered during the 1840s, saw its fortunes tied increasingly to the Ontario wheat economy. On the other hand, the forestry sector, supporting a few small towns in both provinces as well as Bytown and Quebec City, had proven to be a much less potent generator of urban growth.

45 Blanchard, *Le centre du Canada français*, 320
46 Blanchard, *L'ouest du Canada français*, 144
47 Bouchette, *British Dominions*, I, 210, 305-6
48 Raoul Blanchard, *L'est du Canada français*, 2 vols. (Montreal 1935), I, 177

6
Transportation

Although the early roads of Ontario received a very bad press, recorded complaints were generally voiced by British travellers of aristocratic origin. As early as 1817 rural residents had expressed mild praise for the serviceability of the roads in their submissions to an investigation conducted by Robert Gourlay. Roads were adequate for the wheat farmer because most produce was either transported to the lake ports by sleigh in the winter or sold to the inland millers. Because time for winter land-clearing was at a premium, the farmer frequently chose the latter course of action despite the higher prices received at the ports.[1]

Road-building was very much the affair of individual farmers, private businessmen, and municipal governments. Especially after 1840, the role of provincial government expenditures was minimal.[2] Farmers and joint stock companies built roads if the anticipated exportable surplus and associated imports were sufficient to justify the cost, while the very *raison d'être* of Ontario towns was based on their ability to tap the agricultural hinterland. Roads, therefore, were much more the result than the cause of the economic opportunity provided by the wheat economy.

1 The information in this paragraph is from Thomas F. McIlwraith, 'The Adequacy of Rural Roads: An Illustration from Upper Canada,' *Canadian Geographer* xiv, 4 (1970), 344-60, who based his conclusions on a detailed analysis of York County between 1790 and the 1850s.
2 Between 1791 and 1861 the provincial government spent a total of $3.5 million on roads. To place it in perspective, this sum, covering a period of seventy years, was equal to about one-quarter of the value of the wheat crop of 1851 and to one-sixth of the value of colonial expenditures on canals and other navigation works over the same period. By contrast, in the two decades after the Union of 1841, municipalities and joint stock companies spent $4.4 million on roads, *excluding* all roads made by statute labour or commutation money and all municipal outlays on common roads. H.Y. Hind *et al.*, *Eighty Years' Progress of British North America* (Toronto 1863), 127, 177-8

A typical example is provided by the village of Oakville which numbered only 300 inhabitants in 1836 and just short of 1000 in 1850. In the 1830s the main concession roads were built by the settlers, secondary roads were opened by statute labour, and only the main Lake Shore Road was built by the provincial government. In the next decade a joint stock company was formed to build a sixty-mile road between Oakville and Fergus. Of a total stock subscription of £7000, £2000 was subscribed by individuals living in the townships through which the road was to pass, £2000 was received from the township council, and £3000 was received from the county council[3] Such examples are almost as numerous as the towns of mid-century Ontario, and for the province as a whole the great majority of funds for road-building originated at the local level. The government-sponsored colonization roads of the 1850s were the one important exception to this generalization, but they were a fiasco because 'just as the making of these roads was well under way, the good land came to an end.'[4]

The first major canal was the Rideau. Built by the imperial government for military reasons, it was never of much significance for Ontario agriculture. The Welland Canal conferred significant cost savings on farmers to the west, although it was viewed with scepticism by those who feared American competition.[5] For the province as a whole, the most important waterways were the St Lawrence canals and the Erie Canal. The St Lawrence canals were built mainly in the 1840s and their major effect on freight rates was not felt until 1848.[6] By that time the second American Drawback Act, which permitted Canadian produce to pass through the United States in bond, had given Ontario farmers free access to the American route to Britain via the Erie Canal. The St Lawrence canals therefore offered little advantage to the

3 Hazel C. Mathews, *Oakville and the Sixteen: The History of an Ontario Port* (Toronto 1953), 193

4 H.A. Innis and A.R.M. Lower, *Select Documents in Canadian Economic History, 1783-1885* (Toronto 1933), 54. George W. Spragge, 'Colonization Roads in Canada West, 1850-1867,' *Ontario History*, XLIX (1957), 1-17, gives a detailed account of the failure of these roads.

5 Hugh G.J. Aitken, *The Welland Canal Company* (Cambridge, Mass. 1954), 121-2; D.G. Creighton, *The Commercial Empire of the St. Lawrence, 1760-1850* (Toronto 1937), 269-71

6 The freight on a barrel of flour from Hamilton or Toronto to Montreal was about 4 s. in the mid-1820s, 2 to 3 s. in the early 1840s, and 1 s. to 1 s. 6 d. after 1848. T.W. Acheson, 'The Nature and Structure of York Commerce in the 1820s,' in J.K. Johnson, ed., *Historical Essays on Upper Canada* (Carleton Library no 82, 1975), 184; D.L. Burn, 'Canada and the Repeal of the Corn Laws,' *Cambridge Historical Journal*, II (1928), 270; G.P. de T. Glazebrook, *A History of Transportation in Canada*, 2 vols. (Carleton Library no 11, 1964), I, 93

TABLE 6.1
Railways in Quebec and Ontario, 1861 and 1871

	Mileage opened by January 1861		Mileage opened by 1 January 1871	
	Quebec	Ontario	Quebec	Ontario
Grand Trunk Mainline	405	465	405	465
Great Western Mainline		229		229
Other	150	658	317	747
Total	555	1352	722	1441

Source: Hind *et al.*, *Eighty Years' Progress of British North America*, 193-4, and M.L. Bladen, 'Construction of Railways in Canada to the Year 1885,' *Contributions to Canadian Economics*, v (1932), 43-60

Ontario farmers on shipments to Britain, although they represented a cost saving on wheat sold in Quebec and the Maritimes.[7]

Thus, roads were merely a consequence of more basic factors, and Canadian canals, so crucial to the aspirations of the Montreal merchants, were much less important from the point of view of Ontario farmers. Indeed, it can be argued that the most important development for Ontario farmers was the Erie Canal, for it prevented Montreal from monopolizing the benefits from improvements to the St Lawrence system, and it was a major factor in Ontario's emerging independence from that city. Nevertheless, the combination of the Drawback Act and the St Lawrence canals was undoubtedly a significant factor in the growth of wheat exports during the 1840s.

After 1850 Ontario entered the railway age. In that year the province had no railways, but by 1871 over 1400 miles of track had been opened (Table 6.1). Construction was highly concentrated in the four-year period 1853-56, during which a thousand miles were completed. By the end of the period the province had two major east-west lines, the Grand Trunk and the Great Western. Railways led north from Brockville, Prescott, Port Hope, Cobourg, Toronto (two), Hamilton, Galt, Port Dover, and Port Stanley. Branch lines criss-crossed Ontario west of Toronto.

The coming of the railway increased the potential size of each town's hinterland, but the visions of Ontario railway promoters were generally confined

7 In the case of the Maritimes, however, a significant and growing volume of Ontario flour arrived there via New York in bond. I.D. Andrews, *Report on the Trade and Commerce of the British North American Colonies and upon the Trade of the Great Lakes and Rivers* (Washington 1853), 435

to the territory of their own province. Only in exceptional cases was the trade of the American west a major factor in Ontario-based railway construction. American produce was certainly a key consideration in the construction of the Grand Trunk Railway, but this was an enterprise controlled in Britain and Montreal. Also, the Great Western was designed in part for American traffic, but the value of local freight was considerably greater than the value of foreign freight.[8] The great majority of the other railways of Ontario, making up over half of the province's mileage, depended exclusively on outward shipments of Ontario-produced commodities and inward shipments of goods for consumption in the province. Thus, as in the case of roads, the economic base of the railways was firmly rooted in the Ontario wheat economy.

While the stakes had become higher, in many respects the basic nature of the game did not change with the shift from roads to railways. The growth of towns continued to depend on penetration of the agricultural hinterland, and the shift from roads to railways represented merely a technologically based change in the form of that penetration. In both cases the object was to control the imports and exports of the maximum possible territory, and in both cases the energy behind the transportation projects originated in the merchants and municipal governments of the rival towns.

In Toronto both merchants and patricians had become personally committed to building the Northern Railway by 1850,[9] and added to individual commitments were the contributions of local governments. The city of Toronto contributed at least $300,000 to railway projects during the 1850s and 1860s, and smaller bodies such as the Simcoe District council also subscribed funds.[10] In Hamilton and London a group of merchants led by Sir Allan MacNab had obtained a charter for the London and Gore Railroad Company as early as 1834. This company later became the Great Western, and around 1850 it received stock subscriptions of £25,000 each from Oxford County, Middlesex County, Galt, and London. Hamilton bankrupted itself by subscribing £100,000 to the Great Western and £110,000 to local lines.[11] Many other townships, counties, and towns lent or gave money

---

8 Russell D. Smith, 'The Early Years of the Great Western Railway, 1833-1857,' *Ontario History*, LX (1968), 222

9 Barry D. Dyster, 'Toronto, 1840-1860: Making It in a British Protestant Town,' unpublished PHD thesis, University of Toronto, 1970, pp. 306-7

10 Donald C. Masters, *The Reciprocity Treaty of 1854* (London 1936), 67; Dyster, *ibid*, 307; Jacob Spelt, *Urban Development in South-Central Ontario* (Carleton Library no 57, 1972), 113

11 Marjorie Freeman Campbell, *A Mountain and a City: The Story of Hamilton* (Toronto 1966), 110, 120, 134-5; Smith, 'Great Western,' 211

to railways, and funds were also derived directly from the farmers. In the words of Barry Dyster, 'Massive or ambitious funding of financial institutions was rarely attempted [in Toronto], and when it was achieved as in the case of the Bank of Toronto, the major part of the money came from the countryside behind the city. It was to this fertile hinterland that the new finance companies turned as well.'[12]

While the leading merchants and local governments provided the driving force behind railway construction, they nevertheless provided only a relatively small fraction of the money. Railways required capital on a scale that was well beyond the capacity of Canada to provide, and most of this capital was ultimately of external origin. The cost of Canadian railroads and equipment as of 1 January 1861 consisted of the following:[13]

Grand Trunk Railway	$ 56 million
Great Western Railway	23 million
Other Ontario lines	22 million
Other Quebec lines	6 million
Total	$107 million

Apart from government assistance, the Grand Trunk was financed in Britain, and most of the capital for construction of the Great Western originated in the United States. The government of the Province of Canada contributed a total of just over $20 million to these two railways and to the Northern, and in addition it guaranteed $6.5 million in loans to municipalities for railway construction. Including contributions of municipalities that acted on their own credit, the public sector contributed about $30 million to railway construction, although Britain was the ultimate source of most of this as well.[14]

Thus, railway construction depended on foreign capital, and foreign capital was forthcoming on the premise that railway-generated agricultural traffic would earn enough foreign exchange to service the debt. It was no accident, therefore, that construction was concentrated in the peak years of the wheat boom, for the traffic of these years fully supported the optimistic expecta-

12 Dyster, 'Toronto,' 292
13 Hind et al., *Eighty Years' Progress* 195. The total figure of $97.2 million given in this source excludes a number of smaller lines, and it was assumed that the cost per mile for the lines excluded was the same as the average for all other lines.
14 The financing of the Grand Trunk is described in *ibid.*, 197-214; the financing of the Great Western in Smith, 'Great Western,' and in Hind, *ibid.*, 229-36. On government contributions, see *ibid.*, 192, 195, 215-17.

tions on which the supply of foreign capital depended. In its early years the Great Western was a widely reported financial success, declaring dividends of 8 per cent in 1855 and 8.5 per cent in 1856,[15] and in the opinion of Thomas C. Keefer it was this success which allowed the completion of the other Canadian railways:

The great success which attended the early years of the Great Western assisted every other Canadian road, and was doubtless the main instrument in preventing the Grand Trunk from being prematurely abandoned. Whatever loss of prestige or character the province [of Canada] may suffer from the almost universal failure of her railways, as investments, it is clear that in a material sense she has been benefited immensely by the early luck of the Great Western, and by the English infatuation about Grand Trunk; for without these the means for the construction of many miles now in use would not have been raised. The construction of the other lines simultaneously with Grand Trunk was equally opportune, because there would have been little prospect of getting them done after the bankruptcy of that road.[16]

In a double sense, then, Ontario's railway construction flowed from the growth of the wheat economy. On the one hand, this construction was merely a technological extension of the inter-urban competition which had preceded the railway age. On the other hand, the means for this competition, now well beyond the resources of Ontario residents, was forthcoming on the expectation that the wheat boom of the mid-1850s would continue in the future. That it did not was unfortunate for the British and American investors, but Ontario had her railways nevertheless.

In contrast with Ontario railways, most Quebec-based lines were designed to transport goods produced *outside* the province of Quebec. Both the Grand Trunk and the Montreal and Champlain were built in an attempt to strengthen Montreal's position in the competition for the trade of the American and Canadian west. Neither railway had much to do with goods produced in Quebec. Yet, excluding these two railways, Quebec had only 68 miles of track in 1861 and, after the construction of a few short lines connecting the Eastern Townships to the United States, 235 miles in 1871. This compares with close to a thousand miles in Ontario excluding the Grand Trunk. Also, by 1861 Quebec municipalities had borrowed only one-fifth as much as Ontario municipalities from the Municipal Loan Fund,[17] which had been established to assist with the financing of local railways.

15 Smith, *ibid.*, 222
16 Cited in Hind *et al.*, *Eighty Years' Progress*, 221
17 *Ibid.*, 216-17

These differences in the amount and pattern of railway construction in the two provinces were merely another aspect of the divergent patterns of urban growth, which in turn flowed from differences in the agricultural sector. In Quebec there were fewer towns to connect to each other, and the lower level of trade in agricultural commodities implied lower volumes of potential traffic as well as a weaker basis for urban development. The availability of capital may also have been a factor to the extent that the smaller lines in Ontario depended upon locally generated funds, but the existence of the Municipal Loan Fund suggests that differences in potential traffic were the main factor behind the divergent patterns of railway construction. Both factors, of course, depended ultimately on the productivity of agriculture.

The railways had decisive effects on the rise and fall of Ontario towns. The railway network resolved the conflict between Port Hope and Cobourg in favour of the latter, and it brought stagnation to many of the old wheat ports, particularly those such as Oakville and Port Credit, which were located between Toronto and Hamilton. Oakville was said to have reached its zenith in 1860.[18] Russell D. Smith provides an account of the manner in which 'new towns and villages were created, and existing towns and villages were given new life as industries gravitated towards those places served by the [Great Western] railway.' Towns not located along the railway lost population. Douglas McCalla describes how Hamilton declined as a wholesale centre as the opening of the Grand Trunk west of Toronto provided half of Hamilton's customers with superior access to Toronto.[19] In general Toronto was strengthened by its position as a railway centre. Also, it has been seen that some Quebec towns benefited from their location on a railway line, although such towns were few in number.

In the long run the railways tended to favour the centralization of urban activity. However, their effects in this respect were not great in the years up to 1870, for it has been seen that urban concentration was no greater in 1870 than in 1850 in either province. In these early years railways induced more a reshuffling of the urban population than a marked tendency towards its concentration. More important were the effects of the railways on industrial development. Railways allowed manufacturers to reach wider markets, they broke down the natural protection offered by high transport costs, and they created a demand for railway-related equipment. While these matters are taken up in the next chapter, the point to be emphasized here is that transportation advances followed the same general lines as urban and commercial

18 Spelt, *Urban Development*, 111-12, 115, 135-6; Mathews, *Oakville and the Sixteen*, 333
19 Smith, 'Great Western,' 225-7; McCalla, 'The Decline of Hamilton as a Wholesale Center.' *Ontario History*, LXV (1973), 247-54

development. In Ontario development was relatively generalized, and it was based mainly on the local production of wheat and the linkages tht flowed from wheat. In Quebec, activity in Montreal was based on production occurring outside the province, and elsewhere in Quebec there was little activity at all.

7
Industrial development, 1850-70

In neither province had industrial development proceeded much beyond the artisan stage by 1850. The great majority of enterprises employed less than five people, and in the whole country only a handful of firms had as many as a hundred employees. More than three-quarters of those engaged in industrial occupations lived outside the seven largest towns of Quebec and Ontario. The most important occupations were related to apparel (textiles, clothing, and footwear), blacksmithing, and the staple trades (flour milling and lumber). In both provinces these three categories alone accounted for about 70 per cent of the industrial work force.[1] Specialization was rare, for occupational structure showed little variation among the major urban centres, and there were few cases in which as many as half of the members of an occupation were located in the major towns.

This small-scale, dispersed industry was predominant even in the largest urban centres. Several authors have commented on Toronto's modest progress in manufacturing before 1850, and the occupational structure of 1851 was very similar to that of 1833.[2] Manufacturing had made some progress in

---

1 The derivation and definition of the industrial work force are described in the statistical appendix, which also contains tables giving the occupational breakdown for 1851, 1860, and 1870 (Tables S.7 and S.8).
2 Donald C. Masters wrote that in 1850 'Toronto was still purely a commercial centre,' and 'Progress in the development of manufacturing was still meagre.' Referring to the 1850s, Douglas McCalla wrote: 'Trade, of course, was the primary way to fortune in Toronto; relatively few other avenues to wealth and business and social leadership existed.' Masters, *The Rise of Toronto, 1850-1890* (Toronto 1947), 13; McCalla, 'The Commercial Politics of the Toronto Board of Trade, 1850-1860,' *Canadian Historical Review*, L, 1 (1969), 53. The comments of Jacob Spelt have been mentioned above (p. 60). The occupational structure in 1833 is given in Edith G. Firth, ed., *The Town of York, 1815-1834* (Toronto 1966), xxxii-iii.

Hamilton, but in 1851 only thirty of the city's 282 business establishments employed between six and ten people, and 'but a handful' had more than ten. In 1851 Montreal apparently had only one manufacturing firm that employed more than 100 workers and five employing more than 25. The only major industry where large-scale production had developed by 1850 was shipbuilding, and seven shipyards in Quebec City employed a total of over 1300 men.[3] Thus, manufacturing in the modern sense of the word was virtually non-existent in mid-nineteenth-century Canada.

The following two decades saw significant industrial development, and while both provinces participated in that development the causes and characteristics of industrial growth in Quebec differed markedly from the experience of Ontario.

OVERVIEW OF INDUSTRIAL DEVELOPMENT

It will by now be apparent that an understanding of the economic development of Quebec requires a sharp distinction between the two major cities and the rest of the province. This was true in the areas of urban growth, commerce, and transportation, and it is equally true for industrialization. Until this point the urban population has been defined as those living in centres with population exceeding a thousand. However, the industrial statistics provide separate information only for the two largest cities of Quebec and for the five largest cities and towns of Ontario (Toronto, Hamilton, Kingston, Ottawa, and London). Consequently, in this chapter the 'metropolitan' regions of the two provinces are defined as comprising these seven cities, and the remainder of each province is designated 'non-metropolitan.'[4]

With respect to the size and growth of industry, in all three census years (1851, 1860, 1870) the industrial work force made up about one-quarter of the total working population in both metropolitan regions; over the twenty years it rose from 5.4 per cent to 7.3 per cent in non-metropolitan Quebec and from 11.4 per cent to 12.1 per cent in non-metropolitan Ontario. According to this criterion, by the end of the period non-metropolitan Ontario was about two-thirds more industrialized than non-metropolitan Quebec. By 1870 non-metropolitan Ontario accounted for 44 per cent of the value added

3 Michael Katz, 'The People of a Canadian City: 1851-2,' *Canadian Historical Review*, LIII, 4 (1972), 408, 410; Jean Hamelin and Yves Roby, *Histoire économique du Québec, 1851-1896* (Montreal 1971), 262

4 The numbers reported in this section are based on Tables S.7 to S.10 in the statistical appendix.

of the two provinces, followed by metropolitan Quebec (22 per cent), non-metropolitan Quebec (19 per cent), and metropolitan Ontario (15 per cent).

Another measure of the degree of industrialization is per capita value added in manufacturing. By this criterion, in 1870 non-metropolitan Ontario was about 60 per cent more industrialized than non-metropolitan Quebec. On the other hand, metropolitan Quebec was 13 per cent more industrialized than metropolitan Ontario, and the difference between Montreal and metropolitan Ontario was 38 per cent. The calculation of per capita value added in 1870 for each of the 173 counties of Quebec and Ontario yields a stark contrast between the two provinces. In Quebec there was a small degree of industrial concentration in the vicinities of Montreal, Sherbrooke, Quebec City, and Hull (mainly sawmills), but in the rest of the province there was virtually nothing. On the other hand, industrialization was substantial along the entire length of the northern shores of Lake Erie and Lake Ontario. While generally rather thin, this band formed a solid block in the Hamilton-London region, and reached as far north as Georgian Bay above Toronto and as far north as Ottawa above Kingston.

There were also marked variations in industrial structure and degree of specialization. The occupational structures of the two metropolitan regions were remarkably similar in 1851. However, by 1870 Montreal and Quebec City practised a degree of specialization that was unmatched in any other region. In five major industries, metropolitan Quebec accounted for over half of the combined value added of the two provinces. These were sugar refineries (100 per cent), tobacco products (77 per cent), furriers and hatters (76 per cent), boots and shoes (54 per cent), and shipyards (50 per cent). In metropolitan Ontario only two industries, printing (44 per cent) and meat curing (35 per cent), accounted for as much as 35 per cent of the value added of Quebec and Ontario.[5] Furthermore, while the five key industries of metropolitan Quebec made up 37 per cent of the region's value added, the two industries in which metropolitan Ontario was relatively specialized contributed only 10 per cent of regional value added. In the non-metropolitan regions occupational structure was much more diversified in Ontario than in Quebec. In non-metropolitan Quebec blacksmiths and leather workers made up at least half of the industrial working population in all three census years, while sawmills and flour mills accounted for 40 per cent of value added in 1870.

---

5 Since value added in metropolitan Ontario was about 70 per cent of that of metropolitan Quebec, an industry in the former region which accounted for 35 per cent of the value added of the two provinces may be said to display the same degree of specialization as an industry in the latter region which accounted for 50 per cent.

In 1870 median productivity[6] (as measured by value added per worker) was 36 per cent higher in non-metropolitan Ontario than in non-metropolitan Quebec. Productivity was highest in metropolitan Quebec, especially Montreal, and consequently the spread between urban and rural productivity was much greater in Quebec (72 per cent) than in Ontario (21 per cent).

Finally, wage rates had always been lower in Quebec than in Ontario. In 1836 William Evans wrote that wages were one-quarter to one-third higher in the upper province, and four years earlier William Dunlop had stated that the price of labour was cheaper in the eastern portion of the colony than the west because of proximity to French Canadians, who worked for wages not much, if at all, higher than those of a labourer in England. In 1854 Ontario bricklayers and masons were paid between one-third and two-thirds more than their Quebec counterparts, while unskilled workers in Ontario were paid slightly more than most tradesmen in Quebec.[7] Thus, the wage differential appears to have been substantial since at least the early 1830s and its continuation in the years to 1870 is confirmed by the census. In that year the median wage rate was 57 per cent higher in non-metropolitan Ontario than in non-metropolitan Quebec, while the differential between the two metropolitan regions was 15 per cent in favour of Ontario.

To summarize, in 1870 the region furthest advanced along the road to industrialization was metropolitan Quebec and especially Montreal. With superior levels of productivity and a unique degree of specialization, the region accounted for just over one-fifth of the industrial production of both provinces. By contrast, industry in non-metropolitan Quebec was distinguished by its relative absence and, for such industry as existed, by extremely low levels of both productivity and wage rates. Industry in Ontario was much more homogeneous. The five major towns accounted for only one-quarter of the province's industrial production, and urban-rural differences in indus-

---

6 Median productivity and wage rates for Quebec and Ontario in 1870 are based on the twenty-three industries which employed over 1000 people in one province and at least 500 in the other province. For the regional medians, the same twenty-three industries were examined but five were eliminated because production was insignificant in at least one of the four regions.

7 Evans, *Supplementary Volume to a Treatise on the Theory and Practice of Agriculture* (Montreal 1836), 157; Dunlop, *Statistical Sketches of Upper Canada for the Use of Emigrants* (1832; Toronto 1967), 103; Harold A. Innis and A.R.M. Lower, *Select Documents in Canadian Economic History, 1783-1885* (Toronto 1933), 621. Further evidence on relative wage rates is given in H.C. Pentland, 'Labour and the Development of Industrial Capitalism in Canada,' unpublished PHD thesis, University of Toronto, 1960, 149; and in Norman Macdonald, *Canada: Immigration and Colonization, 1841-1903* (Aberdeen 1968), 367-8.

trial structure, productivity, and wage rates were much less pronounced than in Quebec. With this general picture in mind, we turn now to consider the factors shaping industrial growth in each of the four major regions.

NON-METROPOLITAN QUEBEC AND ONTARIO

The agricultural sector was the fundamental force behind industrial development in non-metropolitan Quebec and Ontario. In both regions agriculture was the prime determinant of the size of the market, and in both regions it was the major factor determining regional differences in the prices and availability of industrial inputs: labour, raw materials, capital, and transportation facilities.

In both non-metropolitan regions the agricultural population made up about three-quarters of the total population in 1850 and more than three-fifths in 1870. As we have seen, the great majority of urban and commercial activity in Ontario was based on agriculture. In non-metropolitan Quebec such activity was much more modest, but most of the rural lawyers, shop-keepers, priests, and domestic servants were indirectly dependent on the agricultural sector. In short, the economic base of both regions was undeniably and overwhelmingly agricultural.

Consequently, the size of the market in each region was tied directly to the level of agricultural incomes, and from this is derived the fundamental significance of the fact that agricultural cash income per farmer in Quebec averaged one-fifth to one-quarter of the figure for Ontario. From this enormous difference flowed differences in the number and income levels of people living in small towns and providing services to the farm population. These people, adding to the demand for manufactured goods, represented multiplier effects which magnified the direct consequences of differences in agricultural incomes. With the great majority of manufactured goods destined to local markets, the impact of agriculture on market size was undoubtedly the most important factor affecting industrial development in the two regions. In 1870, excluding flour and lumber which were largely exported, manufacturing value added in non-metropolitan Quebec was 37 per cent of value added in non-metropolitan Ontario. The equivalent figure for agricultural cash income was 28 per cent.

The central importance of agriculture was recognized in Ontario, for it was observed in 1873 that: 'Agricultural in its several branches has been, and is now, the foundation on which rests the entire industrial fabric of Ontario. On its prosperity all classes depend – and with a good crop or a bad one, business operations, the abundance of money, and the social comforts of our whole people rise and fall, as do the waters of the sea with the flow and ebb of the tide.'[8] The same comment could have been made of non-metropolitan Quebec, except that by Ontario standards farm incomes were always low and the tide never flowed.

Nowhere is the importance of agricultural cash income more evident than in the case of textiles and clothing. While the average Ontario farm produced declining quantities of cloth and linen after 1850, in Quebec production rose by more than 50 per cent over the twenty-year period. In 1870 production per farm was four times as great in Quebec as in Ontario. According to the census of 1870, Canadian farm production of cloth and linen came to a 'total value closely approximating to that produced by all our large manufactories of textile fabrics together.'[9] Consequently, even if average total consumption of cloth had been the same for Quebec and Ontario farmers, the demand for manufactured cloth or clothing would have been much lower in Quebec. This is reflected in the very small clothing and textile sector of non-metro-politan Quebec, although not, as we shall see, in Montreal.

The agricultural implements industry is another striking case of the direct link between farming and industrial development. Starting in the 1850s there was a substantial increase in the use of agricultural machinery, particularly reapers in Ontario, and by 1871 there were 37,874 reapers and mowers in Ontario and 5149 in Quebec. Agricultural machinery was originally imported from the United States, but increasingly it came to be made in rural Ontario as domestic demand rose.[10] By 1870 value added in this industry was $1.5 million in non-metropolitan Ontario and less than $300,000 in non-metro-politan Quebec.

Conditions on the supply side were also important. In terms of agricultural raw materials, the greater abundance of most agricultural commodities in Ontario, the faster response of Ontario farmers to new market conditions, and the higher quality of some Ontario commodities were all factors promot-ing more processing of agricultural goods in Ontario than in Quebec. In 1870 value added in industries processing agricultural inputs was $9.0 million in non-metropolitan Ontario and $3.6 million in non-metropolitan Quebec (Table 7.1). Ontario's lead was greatest in flour and grist mills ($2.8 million) and wool cloth ($1.6 million). It is obvious that agricultural conditions in combination with transportation economics were responsible for the differ-

8 *Canada Farmer*, Toronto, 15 Jan. 1873, p.9, cited in Robert Leslie Jones, *History of Agriculture in Ontario, 1613-1880* (Toronto 1946), xi

9 Census of Canada, 1870, III,

10 The rise of this industry in Ontario is described by Jones, *History of Agriculture*, 199-202.

TABLE 7.1
Distribution of per capita value added in non-metropolitan Quebec and Ontario, 1870

	Quebec	Ontario	Difference
Forward linkages from agriculture	**$3.52**	**$6.04**	**$2.52**
Flour and grist mills	1.49	2.92	1.43
Wool cloth	.30	1.26	.96
Backward linkages to agriculture	**.44**	**1.40**	**.96**
Final demand linkages	**3.81**	**6.99**	**3.17**
Bakeries	.37	.30	.07
Blacksmiths, etc.	1.54	1.73	.19
Carriages	.61	1.29	.68
Clothing	.35	1.28	.93
Furniture, doors, etc.	.20	1.05	.85
Printing	.08	.26	.18
Shoes	.66	1.08	.42
Iron and steel products	**.86**	**2.23**	**1.37**
Unclassified	**2.08**	**2.56**	**.48**
Sawmills and oil refineries	**4.19**	**4.50**	**.31**
Total per capita value added	14.90	23.72	8.82
Population (thousands)	1025	1489	464
Total value added ($ millions)	15.3	35.3	20.0

Forward linkage industries include flour and grist mills, wool cloth, breweries, carding and fulling mills, cheese factories, cider, distilleries, meat curing, preserved foods, tanneries, and tobacco. Backward linkage industries include agricultural implements and saddle and harness making.
Source: statistical appendix, pp. 131, 138, and Census of Canada, 1871

ence in the case of flour. There is evidence that quality was an important factor for wool and meat curing, although Quebec's higher farm production of cloth was also a factor in the former case and imports of hogs from Chicago were important in the case of meat.[11] Also, some Quebec industries processing agricultural raw materials were based on imports. This was almost entirely the case for the tobacco industry and partially true for tanneries and breweries.[12] These were industries that developed in spite of local agricul-

11 Robert Leslie Jones, 'French-Canadian Agriculture in the St. Lawrence Valley, 1815-1850' (1942), in W.T. Easterbrook and M.H. Watkins, eds., *Approaches to Canadian Economic History* (Carleton Library no 31, 1967), 119-20, and 'The Agricultural Development of Lower Canada, 1850-1867,' *Agricultural History*, XIX (1945), 220; Hamelin and Roby, *Histoire économique*, 277
12 Hubert LaRue, *Etudes sur les industries du Québec* (Quebec City 1870), 5-6; Hamelin and Roby, *ibid.*, 277

tural conditions. Consequently, although it is not always possible to determine the importance of the availability of agricultural raw materials relative to local demand conditions, the former was certainly crucial to flour milling and significant in other cases.

Before considering the roles of the supply of labour and capital, the above analysis may be cast in terms of the forward, backward, and final demand linkages of the staple approach: forward linkage industries are those processing agricultural raw materials, backward linkage industries are those producing intermediate inputs for use in the agricultural sector, and final demand linkage industries produce goods consumed by farmers. Table 7.1 provides data on per capita value added in these sectors. Sawmills and oil refineries were clearly based on non-agricultural raw materials, and so are listed separately. Iron and steel products are also listed separately because the source of Ontario's lead was divided amongst backward linkages, final demand linkages, and raw material availability. Such classifications are bound to be arbitrary to some extent, but it is clear from the table that Ontario's lead was very substantial in almost every case, and that the great majority of the difference is explained by the market and the raw materials provided by the agricultural sector.

This, however, is not a complete picture, for by 1870 a number of firms outside the major cities operated on a large scale and produced manufactured goods for sale outside the local area. These enterprises were not based primarily on non-agricultural raw materials, and neither can their development be fully explained in terms of the linkages flowing from agriculture. Such firms were much more numerous in non-metropolitan Ontario than in Quebec, and the dynamics of their growth were very different in the two regions.

Some of the larger enterprises in non-metropolitan Ontario included foundries at Dundas, Newcastle, Cobourg, Oshawa, and Chippewa; woollen mills at Thornburg, Cobourg, and Streetsville; knitting mills at Paris; and cotton mills at Dundas. Americans also established a number of firms during this period, including Cossitt's Agricultural Works and Raymond Sewing Machines, both at Guelph.

In non-metropolitan Ontario the linkages flowing from agriculture had spawned numerous manufactories, and a few of these evolved into larger-scale enterprises. This process is described by Jacob Spelt:

Some of the small service industries grew into larger establishments. This largely depended on the personal initiative of the owner of the workshop or mill. Personal initiative made a blacksmith shop into a foundry and the foundry into an engine and machine factory, or pushed the saw and gristmills into production for wider markets as soon as opportunities arose.

A local sawmill began to cut for the American market; a small flour mill turned to the production of flour for the British consumer; a local tannery grew into a leather and shoe factory selling its products Ontario wide. Most of the agricultural implement factories ... began as small local blacksmiths and repair shops.[13]

Ontario provided fertile ground for this classic pattern of industrial growth. Out of the hundreds of blacksmiths who repaired imported farm machinery, for some reason Arnold Massey started to manufacture the machinery himself, thereby establishing a firm that was to become a major world producer of farm machinery. Out of the hundreds of Ontario shopkeepers, G. McLaughlin happened to leave his shop and set up a carriage factory in Oshawa which later became the first Canadian automobile manufacturer. It is not the individual cases that are significant, since individual successes and failures depended on luck, personal initiative, and a host of other random factors. Rather, the important point is that the wheat economy provided a solid home base for the operation of this process of natural selection.

The wheat trade provided the growing farm incomes and sustained the expanding urban population that constituted the market for industrial goods. Wheat had inspired the improvements in transportation that permitted the local manufacturers to reach a wider market. It was the growth of the wheat economy that had first drawn merchants and artisans to Ontario, and then provided the environment in which they were able to accumulate the capital and experience necessary to expand their operations. Thus, the wheat economy provided all the necessary ingredients for an evolutionary pattern of industrial development based on the internal market, internal sources of capital, internally generated transportation facilities, and locally produced raw materials.

Non-metropolitan Quebec had none of this. Its farmers were much closer to self-sufficiency, and towns were small and few. The region's internal railway network was virtually non-existent. It had repelled rather than attracted artisans from outside the region, and it provided no base for internally generated capital accumulation. Ontario's organic, locally generated, industrial growth was not possible in non-metropolitan Quebec. There was, however, another route to industrial development, a route founded on cheap local

13 Spelt, *Urban Development in South-Central Ontario* (Carleton Library no 57, 1972) 76-7, 126-8

labour in combination with external markets, capital, transportation facilities, and raw materials. This was the path of enclave industrialization, and this was the path followed in non-metropolitan Quebec.

Several enterprises of this type had been established by 1870. As early as 1842 a large woollen factory, with capital of $25,000 and annual produce worth about $36,000 was established by a Mr Lomas in Sherbrooke. In 1856 almost all the goods produced by this firm were sold in Montreal. The largest Canadian paper mill was established at Portneuf in 1840 at a cost of £25,000. In 1856 most of the raw materials of rags, chemicals, etc., came from Montreal, and just under half of production was sold in Ontario, the remainder finding a market in Montreal and Quebec City. A Beauharnois paper mill sold two-thirds of its production in Ontario and a Sherbrooke mill sold almost all of its output in Montreal. Andrew Paton manufactured tweeds at Galt in 1858, but he moved to Sherbrooke in 1866 and established the largest and most modern woollen mill in Canada. The capital cost was $400,000, and the mill employed 500 workers. Wool for the manufacture of tweeds was imported from Australia, New England, and South America, while 'laine du pays' was used for flannel-making. Dominion Cotton Mills and the Montreal Cotton Company were established in the early 1870s in Hochelaga and Valleyfield. These were very large enterprises which employed the most modern technology and sold their products throughout the country. The Montreal Cotton Company was said to pay the lowest wages in the province.[14]

All of these firms started on a large, technically advanced scale. They invariably depended on external markets and capital, and frequently on externally provided raw materials as well. They were drawn to rural Quebec by the cheapness and 'docility' of the local labour, together with the development of transportation facilities to ship in the materials and ship out the finished product. However, partly because of the commanding position of Montreal, such firms were few in number, and their existence did not alter the fact that very little industrial development had occurred in non-metropolitan Quebec.

METROPOLITAN QUEBEC

It was not surprising that Montreal experienced little industrial growth before 1850. The Quebec market for manufactured goods was limited by

14 Innis and Lower, *Select Documents*, 609; (no author), *Montreal in 1856* (Montreal 1856); 49-50; Hamelin and Roby, *Histoire économique*, 271-3; Raoul Blanchard, *L'ouest du Canada français* (Montreal 1953), 143

the low cash incomes of the farmers and the unhappy circumstances of the rural artisans, merchants, and priests. On the other hand, one might have expected more industrial development based on the Ontario market, cheap local labour, and capital derived from Montreal's position as the commercial centre of Canada. However, in 1850 a large Ontario market was of recent origin, the improved St Lawrence canals were even more recent, and rail connections to Ontario were still to be built. The 1840s were a time of exceptionally low prices of British clothing and other goods, from which the local producer had little tariff protection. American goods, frequently imported illegally at no duty, were also important in the Ontario market. In general, the tumultuous economic and political conditions of the second half of the 1840s were perhaps not conducive to large-scale industrial development. With a little more time and improvements in some of these areas, Montreal manufacturing made considerable progress in the 1850s and 1860s.

That substantial advances occurred in the first half of the 1850s is clear from *Montreal in 1856*, a pamphlet published shortly after the opening of the Grand Trunk Railway. This document provides information on some sixty Montreal firms, and, while the coverage of firms along the Lachine Canal was apparently fairly complete, 'information was received from only a few of the numerous, and, in many instances, extensive Factories in town.' Thus metal-based and other heavy industry received fuller coverage than clothing, boots and shoes, and other light industry. Nevertheless, the document provides a wealth of information, and it is clear that many Montreal enterprises were geared to export markets, operating on a large scale with modern machinery. Specialization had already developed in several lines.[15]

In boots and shoes, Brown and Childs employed 800 persons, had introduced the 'latest inventions and improvements,' and sold a 'large portion' of its production to places outside Montreal. There were three other boot and shoe companies mentioned (two of them producing rubber footwear), and together they employed 348 workers. One of these had received medals at the Paris Industrial Exhibition, and in another case it was said that the 'manufactures are sold to all parts of Canada, and some, we believe, have been exported to Europe.' The date of establishment of Brown and Childs is not given, but the other three firms were established in 1847, 1853, and 1854.

The document describes twenty-one metal-based companies, and in thirteen cases provides information on employment. Four companies employed between 100 and 250 workers each and sold their products throughout

15 *Montreal in 1856*, 37-8

Canada (and in one case for export). The remainder employed between 30 and 80 workers and in almost every case operated on a Canada-wide basis. Several firms had won prizes at London and Paris exhibitions. Six operations are mentioned in the clothing and textile sector, although this was an area of substantial undercoverage. The largest, Moss and Brothers, employed 800 men and women and sent eleven-twelfths of its production 'abroad.' Two sold half their output for home consumption, and one produced solely for home consumption. Moss and Brothers was established in 1836, and the other five firms were established after 1850. Employment in these five ranged from 43 to 300.

Two furriers, established in 1832 and 1842, employed a total of 190 women and 32 men. One sold one-quarter and the other one-fifteenth of production in the home market. In the area of wood products, a cabinet maker employed 82 and exported 40 per cent of production, and a maker of doors and windows employed 75 and sent half of production to Ontario. A chair factory producing for home consumption employed 25, and a maker of doors and sashes employed 50 to 55. The cabinet maker was established in 1845, and the others commenced operations in 1852 or later.

There were many other miscellaneous enterprises. Redpath Sugar, established in 1855, was the only sugar producer in Canada and employed more than 100. In 1862 the company was said to produce about seven-eighths of the white sugar consumed in Canada.[16] City Flour Mills employed 200 and exported seven-eighths of production. There were four small carriage makers catering to the local market. Twelve tobacco manufacturers imported the raw material from the United States, employed 100 people, and sold half of the finished product in Ontario. Two makers of tobacco pipes employed 120 and sold their products throughout the country. Twelve bookbinders employed a total of about 95 workers, and the only one described (employing 20) sold its products mainly in Ontario.

The foregoing should be adequate to demonstrate the large size of many Montreal firms, their general orientation towards external markets, principally Ontario, and their recent establishment (out of 44 firms, 12 were established before 1845, 8 between 1845 and 1849, and 24 between 1850 and 1855). It is also clear, despite undercoverage, that there was a concentration of production and exports in the areas of footwear, clothing, fur hats, sugar, and certain metal products. Wages appear to have been extremely low in the areas of clothing and fur products and slightly below average in the boot and shoe industry.

16 Samuel Phillips Day, *English America*, 2 vols. (London 1864), I, 190

A final point is the capital intensity of production. Where information was given, buildings were generally made of brick and frequently contained several storeys. Machinery was described in detail and in some cases was said to be extensive or modern. These general comments are supported by the figures on capital investment. Two boot and shoe factories had capital valued at $580 per person employed, as compared with an industry average of $160 for Ontario in 1870. Capital invested amounted to $180,000 for Redpath Sugar, $240,000 for Moss and Brothers, and $200,000 for City Flour Mills. A threshing machine company had invested capital of $148,000, a foundry had $54,000, a door and window factory had $80,000, a furrier had $60,000, and a cabinet maker had $72,000. These figures are large in comparison with an average invested capital per worker of $434 in Ontario fifteen years later. The figures are only rough approximations since the definition of capital is not provided, but the capital intensity of Montreal industry is also indicated by the 1870-71 census. The aggregate ratio of capital to labour was $524 in Montreal, which was 19 per cent higher than in metropolitan Ontario and 22 per cent higher than in Toronto. Figures on invested capital by industry are not available at the sub-provincial level, but taking value added per worker as a proxy Montreal productivity was very high in the three major industries (excluding sugar which was not produced in Ontario) in which metropolitan Quebec specialized most. Thus, for boots and shoes, furriers and hatters, and tobacco, value added per worker in metropolitan Quebec was higher than in metropolitan Ontario by 19, 87, and 81 per cent respectively. The productivity differences in the last two cases were the highest of the eighteen major industries examined. Consequently, at least for the industries in which Montreal specialized, Montreal industry was characterized by large firms using modern technology of a relatively capital-intensive nature.

By the middle of the 1850s the important characteristics of Montreal industry had been established, and these characteristics intensified in the years to 1870. The Victoria Iron Works were established in 1859, and in 1862 the mill employed 120 workers and produced twelve tons of nails per day. The most important raw materials were Scottish pig iron, ore from Port Henry and Lake Champlain, and coal mainly from the Albion mines of New York. This plant, together with one other Montreal puddling and rolling mill, could satisfy the nail requirements of the whole Canadian market.[17] An inquiry of 1864 enumerated seven foundries, and in 1865 three rolling mills and nail works employed a total of 420 skilled workmen and 164 labourers and apprentices. Manufacturers of saws and edge tools employed 200 men.

17 *Ibid.*, I, 180-5

In 1869 William J. Patterson, secretary of the Montreal Board of Trade, counted 12 foundries, 3 rolling mills, and 5 nail manufacturers. Patterson also noted improvements in the past few years in the machinery used by the shoe manufacturers, and he estimated that Montreal firms employed 7000 people and accounted for three-quarters of total Canadian production.[18]

The question, then, is why as early as 1855 Montreal had developed an industrial sector which operated on a Canada-wide basis and on a much larger scale than industry in other Canadian cities. Why was it that a large part of the demand stemming from the Ontario wheat boom was met by manufacturers in Montreal rather than by manufacturers in Ontario towns? Certainly Montreal was favoured by the power provided by the Lachine Canal and the Lachine Rapids, and starting in 1846 many plants were established along the canal. The improvements in the St Lawrence canals by 1848 and the opening of the Grand Trunk Railway to Toronto in 1855 improved the accessibility of the Ontario market. Montreal also had access to relatively low-cost coal, and it was in a favoured position for imports of pig iron from Britain, which was the major supplier of that commodity. However, with the exception of British pig iron, none of these factors explains Montreal's ability to compete successfully in the Ontario market, since a number of locations in that province had equally favourable sources of power and certainly lower transportation costs. Montreal's success relative to Ontario towns should be ascribed mainly to the cheapness of labour, the greater availability of capital in the country's commercial centre, and, in some cases, to the lower cost of overseas imports of raw materials.

On the first point, the analysis of the authors of *Montreal in 1856* is worth reproducing in full:

Another advantage Montreal possesses [in addition to being a commercial city and having access to water power], is found in the density of the population of the surrounding districts. In many places the land has been subdivided until the holdings of each man are too small for profitable agriculture, and the people, deeply attached to the soil, are unwilling to leave the older settlements in the valleys of the St. Lawrence

---

18 Patterson, *Statistical Contributions relating to the Trade, Commerce and Navigation of the Dominion of Canada*, second series (Montreal 1875), 1872 report, 40; Hamelin and Roby, *Histoire économique*, 274-5; Innis and Lower, *Select Documents*, 598. The Census of 1870-71 indicates employment of 5175 and gross production equal to 40 per cent of the total for Quebec and Ontario (Quebec City contributed 15 per cent). However, the census enumerates 3384 producers in the two provinces, whereas Patterson was referring only to manufacturers. For example, he wrote that there were 30 boot and shoe manufacturers in Montreal, as compared with 117 listed in the census.

and Richelieu so long as they can obtain subsistence there ... No where are there found people better adapted for factory hands, more intelligent, docile, and giving less trouble to their employers, than in Lower Canada. Twenty or twenty-five years ago this population was most prosperous in agricultural pursuits; large crops of wheat were grown here, and a considerable surplus exported. The fly came, the wheat crops ceased, and the surplus for export of the coarser grains which have since been grown, has proved less remunerative ... Owing to the causes above alluded to, agricultural wages are not so high here as in those portions of the Province [of Canada] where wheat is more largely grown, and hands can be obtained to work in the factories at more reasonable rates than there ... Here we have abundant water-power, and cheap and abundant labour.

It is critical to an understanding of the nature of Montreal's industrial development that 'the density of the population of the surrounding districts' was seen as an advantage because it represented a supply of cheap labour and not because it constituted a market for manufactured goods. This, of course, is in sharp contrast to the role of the agricultural hinterlands of Toronto, Hamilton, and other Ontario towns. The size of the market was a vital concern of Montreal manufacturers, and, according to the authors of *Montreal in 1856*, 'The sole difficulties with which they [Montreal manufacturers] have to contend are a restricted market, and the competition of the larger, wealthier, and longer established factories in other countries.' It was the restricted size of the *Canadian* market to which the authors referred. Montreal manufacturers looked to the local countryside for their labour, and they looked to the country as a whole for their market.

The authors also noted the connection between local agriculture and the level of wages. In a situation where the bulk of the agricultural work force was made up of owners of land rather than landless farm labourers, incomes were tied securely to agricultural productivity.[19] Consequently, the opportunity cost of accepting wage employment was much greater for the agricultural population of Ontario than for that of Quebec. Furthermore, despite the practice of subdivision of land on inheritance in Quebec (which created further downward pressures on average income levels as observed in the passage just cited), increases in the agricultural population of Quebec could not be absorbed even at a low standard of living. According to one estimate,

---

19 As late as 1875 a British trade unionist remarked that, on the whole, ' farm labour for hire is in Canada only a transient avocation, there being in this country no large body of men who expect to devote their lives to working for wages, as every healthy and sober man can easily become a landholder.' Innis and Lower, *Select Documents*, 535-6

199,000 French Canadians or 24 per cent of the French population of 1861 left the province between 1862 and 1871.[20] Finally, the link between agricultural conditions and industrial wage rates is strengthened by the rapid decline in the relative importance of immigration to Canada from Britain after 1850.[21] All this suggests that the very much higher productivity of Ontario agriculture, together with the greater capacity of that province to absorb increased population, were the major factors behind the wage differential.

It certainly cannot be argued that the lower wages paid in Montreal reflected a shortage of capital in that city. Relative to the cities and towns of Ontario, Montreal had abundant capital *and* abundant labour. It has been seen that both median labour productivity and the aggregate ratio of invested capital to labour were greater in Montreal than in metropolitan Ontario.

As the commercial centre of the country, Montreal had a disproportionate share of the men with sufficient capital to establish large industrial enterprises. True, these men frequently lacked the technical knowledge necessary for industrial development, but they were well placed to enter into partnerships with others, often Americans, who had this knowledge.[22] Thus both the cheapness of labour and the availability of capital were factors favouring the growth of large-scale industry in Montreal. Their early use of modern technology and their relatively low wages allowed Montreal firms to compete effectively in the Ontario market.

The importance of these factors naturally varied from industry to industry, although all exporting industries benefited from the transportation network. Light industries such as boots and shoes and clothing did not use the water power of the Lachine Canal, but both of these industries benefited substantially from low wages. In the case of boots and shoes, the early establishment of large-scale production may also have been an important factor, although such production might not have been profitable had wages been higher. It appears from the census that Montreal's specialization in clothing was not strong in 1870 despite the several large firms in existence in the 1850s. However, there was rapid growth during the 1870s, and in the 1880s it was said that '... the cheapness of labour in Montreal in this line of work cannot be overcome by other markets of the Dominion, hence the future of the industry here will remain, as in the past, unparalled [sic] by any competition from any Canadian source.'[23] The sugar and iron and steel industries benefited

20 Hamelin and Roby, *Histoire économique*, 53, 67
21 Helen I. Cowan, *British Emigration to British North American* (Toronto 1961), 288
22 Innis and Lower, *Select Documents*, 300-1
23 Cited in Hamelin and Roby, *Histoire économique*, 254

from Montreal's location, from the power provided by the Lachine Canal, and from the availability of capital associated with the city, as well as from cheap labour. Therefore, while there were considerable variations from industry to industry, the low wages associated with an unproductive agriculture were undoubtedly a key factor in the development of several of Montreal's most important industries.

The industrial sector of Quebec City may be mentioned briefly. Between 1850 and 1870 the population of Quebec rose at only half the rate of Montreal, or by just under 2 per cent per annum. In 1870 industrial value added in Quebec was just over one-quarter that of Montreal, while industrial employment was about one-third that of Montreal. The most important industries were boots and shoes, tanneries, and shipyards which together made up 41 per cent of the city's value added and 40 per cent of employment. Wood-related industries other than shipbuilding were not particularly large in Quebec. In all of the five major industries (cabinet and furniture, carpenters and joiners, carriages, cooperage, and sawmills), production was greater in Montreal than in Quebec.

It seems that few of the raw materials used by the industries of Quebec City were produced locally. Three-quarters of the hides used by Quebec tanneries came from Ontario and the American west. According to Hubert LaRue, the three Quebec soap and candle factories imported all their soda from Britain and their tallow and fats from Montreal. The quentity of the last two products made in the Quebec district was not sufficient to supply one-tenth of the local industry's needs. By 1870 even the barley used by the city's breweries was imported from the west. The bakeries would have been dependent on western wheat, and the bulk of the wood received at Quebec came from the Ottawa Valley. LaRue stated that many of the difficulties faced by Quebec industry stemmed from the lack of a back country, concluding that: 'Quiconque a fait l'étude de nos industries québécoises a du se convaincre, que ces seuls mots [back country] donnent la clef de bien des énigmes industrielles.' Albert Faucher reached a similar conclusion in his study almost ninety years later.[24]

The head start enjoyed by Montreal, as well as its larger size and superior access to capital and to the Ontario market, also seemed to have adverse effects on Quebec's industrial development. It was said that Quebec's small market as compared with that of Montreal had prevented the manufacture

24 LaRue, *Etudes*, 32-4, 40; Albert Faucher, 'The Decline of Shipbuilding at Quebec in the Nineteenth Century,' *Canadian Journal of Economics and Political Science,* XXIII (1957), 195-215

of better quality soaps, and in 1870 the city bought most of its good soap from Montreal manufacturers. Quebec City brewers had received 'rude competition' from Montreal beer after a plant with all the recent British improvements had been set up in the latter city in the first half of the 1850s. Mechanization of Quebec's boot and shoe industry began in 1864, fifteen years later than in Montreal, under the influence of men who had previously worked in the Montreal industry.[25] Although Quebec was a major producer of leather, the principal Canadian leather market was in Montreal. In brief, then, the industrial development of Quebec City was held back by the absence of an agricultural hinterland and by the success of Montreal. Also, for reasons to be discussed below, wood proved to be an unsatisfactory basis for industrialization.

METROPOLITAN ONTARIO

There is less need to distinguish between the urban and rural sectors of Ontario, since Ontario industry was much more dispersed and homogeneous. Nevertheless, a brief examination of the industrial development of urban Ontario will at least serve to underline the special position held by Montreal, which in 1870 had an industrial value added greater than that of the five Ontario cities combined.

In 1866 Toronto appears to have had at least seven firms employing more than 100 workers.[26] The largest was the cabinet factory of Jacques and Hay, which employed at least 200 in the mid-1850s and 400 in 1866. Toronto Rolling Mills was set up in 1860 to re-roll iron rails. The firm employed 140 in 1860 and 300 in 1866, but along with the Steel, Iron and Railway Works Company it was closed down in 1872-73 as a result of the shift from iron to steel rails. A meat-packing plant also employed 300 in 1866. These appear to have been the three largest enterprises, followed by Gooderham and Worts, distillers (160 workers), a boiler and still establishment (120), and two tobacco manufacturers (150 and 100). However, the census indicates that at least the four largest of these firms offered substantially less employment in 1870 than indicated by the above figures for 1866. The outstanding feature of Toronto's industrial structure in 1870 was its large number of printers and tailors, but in most respects the city's industrial structure was similar to that of Ontario as a whole.

25 LaRue, *Etudes*, 35-9, 44; Hamelin and Roby, *Histoire économique*, 269-70
26 The information in this paragraph is taken from Barry D. Dyster, 'Toronto, 1840-1860: Making It in a British Protestant Town,' unpublished PHD thesis, University of Toronto, 1970, pp. 258-9; Donald C. Masters, *The Reciprocity Treaty of 1854* (London 1936), 61-2; and Innis and Lower, *Select Documents*, 593.

In 1870 industrial production in Hamilton was somewhat less than half that of Toronto. Hamilton was unique in its specialization in metal products, which came to 44 per cent of its total value added of $2.6 million and to just over half the value of production of such goods in Montreal. A major contributor to this sector was the Great Western railway shops which were established in 1859 and expanded to include a rolling mill in 1864. The cost of the plant was a 'staggering' $107,500, and it employed about 130 men.[27] According to H.A. Innis and A.R.M. Lower, the company shared the fate of the Toronto Rolling Mills and closed down with the conversion to steel rails in 1872-73. However, it appears that this closure was temporary, for, according to W.J.A. Donald, the company continued in operation until 1879, at which time it was leased to the Ontario Rolling Mill Company.[28] Other companies in this sector included the Burlington Bay Dock and Shipbuilding Company which made steam engines and other items connected with the manufacture and repair of steamers, the stove factory owned by the Gurney brothers and Alexander Carpenter, and, by 1870, four sewing machine companies including the R.M. Wanzer Company.[29] Sewing machines were of major importance in 1870, accounting for one-third of the city's value added in the metal sector.

The extent to which these industries owed their existence to cheap supplies of coal and iron will be assessed later, but for the moment it might be noted that the enterprises connected with railways and shipping represented natural linkages flowing from the city's commercial activities. Also, Hamilton's position as the major importer and wholesaler centre for one of the most prosperous and fastest growing agricultural hinterlands of the province offered exceptional opportunities for import subsitition. Marjorie Freeman Campbell, for example, describes how Hamilton firms of this period supplied the 'Wentworth yeoman and his family' with suction pumps, sewing machines, 'useful and serviceable Family Carriages,' saddles and harnesses, 'ready-to-wear,' and agricultural implements.[30]

London and Ottawa each had industrial value added of about $1.5 million, as compared with only $630,000 for Kingston. The main observation here concerns the importance of wood products (36 per cent of value added) in Ottawa.

27 Charles M. Johnston, *The Head of the Lake* (Hamilton 1958), 190, 192; Marjorie Freeman Campbell, *A Mountain and a City: The Story of Hamilton* (Toronto 1966), 140; Innis and Lower, *ibid.*, 593, 599
28 Donald, *The Canadian Iron and Steel Industry* (Boston and New York 1915), 61; Innis and Lower, *ibid.*, 593
29 Johnston, *The Head of the Lake*, 192-3; Innis and Lower, *ibid.*, 593
30 Campbell, *A Mountain and a City*, 202-3

In general terms, then, and with the exeption of iron and steel products in Hamilton, metropolitan Ontario displayed neither the specialization nor the scale of operations which were characteristic of Montreal. The timing, causes, and patterns of industrial development were similar in the two Ontario regions. In both cases the bulk of the growth occurred in the 1860s, although census figures may be misleading here, since the Ontario economy had not fully recovered from the recession of 1857 by the time of the 1860 census. Nevertheless, it is not surprising that the newer urban centres of Ontario, preoccupied with the wheat boom and railway-building until 1856 and then hit by a violent recession in 1857, needed more time than Montreal to expand their manufacturing sectors. Also, the forces of concentration, which in later years were to draw firms such as Massey-Harris from the smaller centres to the major cities of Ontario, had not yet come to the fore in 1870.

THE ROLE OF THE FORESTRY SECTOR

Forest-based industry has been mentioned on a number of occasions already. The direct impact of this sector was fairly straightforward, sawmills accounting for 28 per cent of the industrial value added of non-metropolitan Quebec in 1870 as compared with 15 per cent for non-metropolitan Ontario. On an absolute per capita basis, sawmills were of approximately equal importance in the two regions.

The indirect impact of the forest sector was also important. For Quebec and Ontario as a whole, exports of forest products were clearly significant throughout the period, as is evident from Figure 4.2. However, from the foregoing pages it is also evident that wood and wheat varied markedly in their effects on industrial development. Viewed as a staple product, wood, whether in the form of square timber or lumber, was much less effective than wheat as an initiator of urban and industrial growth. The major wood-producing region was the Ottawa Valley, and the major commercial centre of the timber industry was Quebec City. Yet the Ottawa Valley experienced meagre industrial and urban development in comparison with western Ontario, while Quebec City experienced low rates of growth of both population and manufacturing. Toronto, Hamilton, to some extent Montreal, and the scores of smaller towns of western Ontario were the legacy of Ontario wheat. By comparison, the legacy of lumber included Quebec City, Ottawa, to some extent Kingston, Collingwood, Trenton, a few small towns like Renfrew in the Ottawa Valley, and two or three Lake Erie ports which declined rapidly after the local pine had been removed.[31] It is evident that by 1870 urban and industrial growth had become concentrated in the regions made up by the first of these groups, while, in general, the second group experienced modest growth at best. As already noted, the difficulties of Quebec City and Kingston have been attributed by several authors to their poor agricultural hinterlands or back countries.

There were several fairly obvious reasons for the very different linkage effects of these two primary activities. Agriculture was more stable than forestry with respect to geographical location, for in a world where conservation measures were unknown the movement of the forest frontier frequently left towns without function and farmers without markets. Also, on a technological level agriculture was more susceptible to diversification. A wheat producer could diversify his production, and in the lucky circumstances of the 1850s and 1860s considerable agricultural diversification took place. By contrast there were no such technical possibilities in the primary branches of the forestry sector, and, as illustrated by the important case of shipbuilding in Quebec City, diversification in wood-based secondary industries sometimes required the abandonment of the basic commodity itself.[32] Consequently, under the technological and market conditions of the period after 1850, the staple trap loomed larger in forestry than in agriculture. Of course, these conditions were not static and agricultural diversification was by no means guaranteed, as the case of Quebec in the first half of the nineteenth century makes all too clear.

In addition, the distribution of the proceeds from the staple product was very different in the two sectors. Family farming is the classic example of an activity associated with a relatively equal distribution of income, and even the profits from staple transportation and distribution were spread among a large number of towns and placed in the hands of merchants typically operating on a relatively small scale. By contrast, the proceeds of the timber trade were very unequally distributed. According to the traditional argument of the staple approach, the more equal income distribution was associated with a pattern of demand which was more likely to be met from domestic sources. On the other hand, the concentration of the proceeds of the timber trade in

---

31 A.R.M. Lower, in *The North American Assault on the Canadian Forest* (Toronto 1938), 121, wrote: 'Unlike the Lake Ontario ports, most of which have become flourishing towns, these little places on Lake Erie declined after the neighbourhood was stripped of its pine. The north shore is now often nothing but a break-water, a few buildings, and a waste of sand, says a writer in 1906.'

32 The fortunes of this industry are analysed by Faucher, 'Decline of Shipbuilding.'

few hands might conceivably have contributed more to capital formation, but a number of factors militated against this possibility. The harsh but eloquent words of the leading authority on the history of Canada's forest industry make the point very clearly:

As for the British American colonies, what did they get out of their forests? There was much labour provided – most of it of low grade. Probably persons employed in equipping and supplying the camps did well. The forest industries had a great deal to do with the growth of Quebec, Saint John, Ottawa, Pembroke, and smaller places, and some of this growth, judged by its permanence, was healthy. Since most labour was of humble status and much of it French, they provided opportunities for life to French Canadians and increased their numbers. They planted a good many settlers, French and English, on the margins of the Shield and in the Shield, whose chief contribution to the Canadian future was to burn the forests and leave behind them broods of children as the founding stock of the large *poor white* element in Canada. They enriched a considerable number of lumber kings, especially in the City of Ottawa. Most of these families have since, like the baseless fabric of a vision, faded, leaving scarce a rack behind ... It is to be presumed that not all the fortunes they built up were frittered away but that some of them, through other investment, added to the total capital in Canada and helped build up her economy ... Much of the profits from the Canadian lumber industry, perhaps most of them, passed into American hands ...

The Canadian forests contributed to the prosperity of the British timber importer and the enrichment of the American lumberman. Canadians got some crumbs from their own rich table ... It must be concluded that the new colonies got the minimum out of the wreck of their forests.

A staple trade such as the timber trade is essentially an exploitative trade and in it the dice are loaded in favour of the metropolis.[33]

Such words could not be used to describe the wheat trade.

THE ROLE OF IRON AND COAL

According to one influential interpretation of industrialization in Quebec and Ontario, a major factor was Ontario's superior access to iron and coal deposits, and hence its lead over Quebec in metal-based industry.[34] Once again a sharp line must be drawn between Montreal and the rest of Quebec. In 1870

33 A.R.M. Lower, *Great Britain's Woodyard* (Montreal 1973), 249-50
34 Albert Faucher and Maurice Lamontagne, 'History of Industrial Development,' in J.-C. Falardeau, ed., *Essais sur le Québec contemporain* (Quebec City 1953), 23-37

Montreal's value added in iron and steel industries was about the same as that of Toronto and Hamilton combined.[35] For the metropolitan regions as a whole value added was about the same in both provinces. It is true that the *relative* importance of this sector was much greater in metropolitan Ontario than in metropolitan Quebec (23.0 per cent versus 15.4 per cent of total value added), but the relative figures reflect the greater importance of other Montreal industries such as boots and shoes as much as the lesser importance of the iron and steel sector. Particularly if one is concerned mainly with larger enterprises, Montreal was the leading producer in this sector in 1870. W.J.A. Donald wrote that by 1879 Ontario had no pig iron producing plant and no very important rolling mills, while Quebec had a few fairly large rolling mills and three small blast furnaces.[36]

In comparing the two non-metropolitan regions, a very different picture emerges. The population of non-metropolitan Ontario was about 50 per cent above that of non-metropolitan Quebec, but value added in iron and steel was just over three times as great in the former as in the latter region. This difference was particularly great in the area of agricultural implements. However, differentials of similar or greater magnitude occurred in many other industries, including flour and grist mills (factor of 2.9), breweries (3.4), cheese (11), distilleries (none in rural Quebec), dress making (3.8), tailors (6.1), wool making (6.2), saddle and harness making (4.1), carriage making (3.0), cabinet making (7.1), sashes, doors, etc. (8.4), cooperage (12), and printing (4.7). Thus there was nothing striking about the differential in the iron and steel sector, and no special explanation is called for.

A second set of questions concerns accessibility to raw materials. Even if, as seems evident, Montreal did not lag behind Ontario cities in this sector, it

35 The figures for value added in 1870 were as follows (in millions of dollars):

	Blacksmithing	Agricultural implements	Other iron and steel	Total
Montreal	0.1	0.0	2.2	2.3
Toronto	0.0	0.0	1.0	1.0
Hamilton	0.0	0.1	1.1	1.2
Metropolitan Quebec	0.2	0.0	2.5	2.7
Metropolitan Ontario	0.1	0.1	2.6	2.8
Non-metropolitan Quebec	0.9	0.3	0.9	2.1
Non-metropolitan Ontario	1.9	1.4	3.3	6.6
Total Quebec	1.1	0.3	3.3	4.7
Total Ontario	2.0	1.5	5.9	9.4

36 Donald, *Canadian Iron and Steel Industry*, 63

is still possible that the cost of raw materials was greater in Montreal than in Toronto or Hamilton. It would appear, however, that Montreal suffered little if any net raw material cost disadvantage in the years to 1870. First, Montreal benefited from cheap water transport, and in the words of Innis and Lower: 'The importance to the iron industries of coal and cheap water-transport tended to favour localities which had cheap, accessible supplies of coal as in the case of ports on Lake Erie (Port Stanley for London) and on Lake Ontario (Hamilton and Toronto) and on the St. Lawrence (Montreal). The existence of abundant supplies of water-power, coal, and cheap water-transport strengthened the position of Montreal as an industrial centre.'[37]

The importance of water transport is underlined by a map in an article by David F. Walker which shows regional variations in the price of coal in southern Ontario.[38] Depending on railway access and the degree of inter-railway competition, the price of coal twenty or thirty miles from Lake Ontario was 20 to 50 per cent higher than the price at the waterfront. These figures apply to a much later year (1916), but the author points out that the relative advantage of water transport was even greater in earlier years. By contrast, in 1872 the price of Nova Scotia coal delivered to Montreal by the Grand Trunk Railway was 12 per cent higher than the price of American coal delivered to Toronto.[39] It is not certain that this is an accurate indication of the cost differential. It was noted above, for example, that the Victoria Rolling Mills obtained much of its coal from New York.

During this period Montreal appears to have been more favourably located than Ontario cities with respect to supplies of iron ore for blast furnaces and of pig iron for rolling mills. Donald provides a detailed description of the development of blast furnaces to 1879, and while neither province enjoyed much permanent success in this area prior to 1879, Quebec fared somewhat better than Ontario. A few enterprises (such as the St Maurice Forges, the Radnor Forges, the Moisie Iron Company, and various establishments in the township of Marmora) operated intermittently, but in general 'British iron was let in at such prices that it was impossible for the Canadian producer to compete in the Ontario market.' In this respect, Montreal rolling mills enjoyed the advantage of cheaper British pig iron, while the few sizeable Ontario mills seem to have re-rolled iron rails or used scrap metal. As already noted, the substitution of steel for iron caused the termination of the Toronto Rolling Mills and the temporary closure of the Steel, Iron and Railway Works Company of Toronto (in 1872 the latter company merged with the Canada Car

37 Innis and Lower, *Select Documents*, 615-16
38 Walker, 'Transportation of Coal into Southern Ontario,' *Ontario History*, LXIII (1971), 19
39 *Journals of the House of Commons*, XI, app. 4, cited in Albert Faucher, *Quebec en Amérique au XIXe siècle* (Montreal 1973), 176

and Manufacturing Company). The Ontario Rolling Mill Company used scrap iron as its raw material.[40]

In brief, then, by 1870 Montreal was the leading large-scale producer of iron and steel products, and the gap between the two rural regions was not greater than for a wide range of other major industries. While Montreal appears to have suffered from a moderate cost disadvantage relative to Toronto and Hamilton in terms of access to coal, the opposite was the case for access to pig iron for rolling mills. The overall effect on raw material costs is not clear. Thus, for the non-metropolitan regions it would seem reasonable to ascribe interprovincial differences to much the same factors as have been cited for the manufacturing sector as a whole. This is particularly evident in the case of agricultural implements. For the metropolitan regions it would also seem justified to stress factors on the demand side. The major Ontario rolling mills were tied to railway construction and to shipping in the case of the Burlington Bay Dock and Shipbuilding Company, and, as has been noted, the local farm population provided a strong demand for the sewing machines, stoves, and other metal products made in Hamilton and Toronto. Despite his earlier emphasis on raw material supplies, Faucher has recently acknowledged the importance of demand factors, and Donald and Innis and Lower also emphasized the importance of the size of the market and particularly the effect of railway construction.[41] In these early years, then, the location of non-agricultural raw materials was not a critical factor in explaining the divergent patterns of industrial growth in the two provinces.

THE ROLE OF COMMERCIAL POLICY

Tariff policy may be analysed at two levels. On the one hand, it may be asked whether actual tariffs had differential impacts on industrialization in the two provinces. Did the commodity pattern of tariffs favour one province over the

---

40 Donald, *Canadian Iron and Steel Industry*, 41-55, 61, 71
41 Referring to Quebec's iron and steel industry, Faucher, *Québec en Amérique*, wrote: 'Mal située par rapport à la demande dérivée de l'agriculture et de l'industrie, isolée des charbonnages canadiens plus que toute autre province, mal préparée financièrement, frappée depuis longtemps d'incapacité scientifique, la province de Québec pouvait-elle s'adapter au nouvel espace qui s'ouvrait à elle ?' Innis and Lower, *Select Documents*, 594, wrote: 'The demands of the railways were chiefly responsible for building up an industry dependent on the imports of iron from other countries.' According to Donald, *ibid.*, 67-8, the greatest developments prior to 1879 came between 1868 and 1879, and these were 'owing largely ... to the increased demand for railway supplies.' In addition, it should be noted that in 1870 Montreal's rolling mills, unlike those of Toronto and Hamilton, were not directly dependent on railways. The Grand Trunk workshops at Point St Charles do not appear until the census of 1880-81.

other? On the other hand, given that a protectionist policy was adopted more than half a century later in Canada than in the United States, it may be asked whether an earlier adoption of such a policy in Canada would have had differential effects on Quebec and Ontario. The first of these questions is considered briefly now, and the second will be analysed in the context of the American experience.

There were no obvious biases in commercial policy which might have been expected to favour one province over the other. According to D.F. Barnett, the Cayley-Galt tariffs of 1858-59 resulted in significant increases in the effective protection afforded to a wide range of industries. One action that would have favoured Quebec more than Ontario was the imposition of a 25 per cent duty on leather goods. Barnett's test suggests that in this case the tariff increase was significant in promoting import substitution. However, this is the conclusion reached by Barnett for industry in general, and in other cases, such as woollen textiles, the large increase in effective protection would presumably have favoured Ontario. In the case of iron and steel products, Donald suggested that the tariffs of this period had a limited impact on domestic growth, and in any case, to the extent that tariffs did have some effect, the benefits may have accrued to Montreal as much as to Ontario towns.[42] In many cases lines provincial specialization had not yet become fully established, so that, even if particular industries did receive special treatment, the provincial distribution of the resulting benefits would not always be clear. Furthermore, if, as argued by Barnett, the Galt tariff tended to equalize the protection enjoyed by different classes of producers, then the scope for regional biases is reduced correspondingly. In brief, then, while the answer must remain tentative, the onus of proof would seem to lie with anyone wishing to argue that the commodity pattern of pre-Confederation commercial policy conferred disproportionate benefits on one or the other province.

COMPARISON WITH THE AMERICAN EXPERIENCE

The regional patterns of industrial growth in the United States provide striking similarities and contrasts with the Canadian situation. The experience of the American west was very close to that of Ontario. According to Douglass C. North, between 1815 and 1860 'the growth in income of the area and its integration into the national economy came basically from the export outside

42 Barnett, 'The Galt Tariff: Incidental or Effective Protection,' *Canadian Journal of Economics*, IX (1976), 398, 405; Donald, *ibid.*, 65-8

the region of wheat, corn and products derived from these two cereals: flour, meal, livestock products, and whiskey.' The most important changes in the western economy were the surges of western expansion associated with high prices of wheat and corn, the redirection of trade from the south to the east and to Europe, the accelerated shift of population out of self-sufficiency during periods of expansion, and the development of a diversified economic structure. Population rose rapidly, and the region accounted for 13 per cent of national population in 1810 and 38 per cent in 1860. There was also considerable urban and industrial growth. Many small towns and villages 'dotted the West,' and 'locally oriented manufacturing trade and services developed along with the widespread pattern of towns in order to serve the local consuming market.' Urban population made up 4 per cent of the total in 1840, 10 per cent in 1850, and 14 per cent in 1860. North lists five factors which made these developments possible: the broad range of production possibilities which permitted a variety of exports; linkages into food processing, agricultural implements, and other industries; cost reductions as a result of the development of transportation facilities and other infrastructure; the relative equality of income distribution which 'led to a pattern of consumer demand which was the most important immediate influence in the widespread growth of small towns and residentiary industry'; and a positive attitude towards investment in education.[43] The most important difference between this picture and the experience of Ontario was the latter's concentration on a single export crop, a situation that was due partly to differing resource endowments but mainly to market conditions. The west had large consuming markets in the east and the south, while Ontario farmers faced a small domestic market and were forced to concentrate on wheat as the only commodity that could be sold abroad. Despite this difference, the dynamics of growth and the resulting economic structures were very similar in the two regions.

The adjustments forced upon northeastern farmers as a result of western competition have already been examined, and it is clear from that analysis that local agriculture could not have been a major stimulus to northeastern industrialization. Prior to the embargo imposed at the end of 1807, there had been little industrial development in the United States. The revenue tariffs

---

43 North, *The Economic Growth of the United States, 1790-1860* (Englewood Cliffs 1961), 135, 153-5. Information on the American experience is derived mainly from Thomas S. Cochran and William Miller, *The Age of Enterprise* (New York 1942); Victor S. Clark, *History of Manufactures in the United States* (New York 1929); Frank W. Taussig, *The Tariff History of the United States* (New Haven 1936); and North. Quotations are from North.

of the period did not exclude British manufactured goods, and industrial development was limited to industries such as shipbuilding in which transport costs or raw materials were important. There was rapid industrial growth during the period 1808-14 when the total or partial exclusion of British imports resulted in a large increase in the price of manufactured goods. This spurt was short-lived, since British goods re-asserted their position after the return to normal trade conditions, and between 1810 and 1820 manufacturing output declined drastically in every state in the northeast. There was some recovery during the 1820s, but it was during the 1830s that industrial growth accelerated throughout the northeast, and after the 1830s there was a continuing rapid growth of manufacturing.

According to North, 'By all odds, the most important influence on the growth of manufacturing was the growth in the size of the domestic market ... The growing localization of industry, specialization of function, and increasing size of firm were all basically related to the growth in the market, which stemmed from the regional specialization and growth of inter-regional trade beginning after 1815, but was *really* accelerated with the surge of expansion in the 1830's ... The cotton trade was the immediate impetus for this regional specialization, and the growth of cotton income in the 1830's was the most important proximate influence upon the spurt of manufacturing growth of that decade.'[44]

This industrial growth was highly concentrated in the northeast, and several factors are advanced to explain this specialization. The first factor was the growth of large urban centres in the northeast prior to substantial industrialization. As early as 1810 New York and Philadelphia each had a population exceeding 90,000, while Baltimore and Boston each had more than 30,000 people. This development was based on international trade and shipping, activities with multiplier effects which further increased urbanization and the size of the market. A second and related factor was the early development of a northeastern capital market around the cotton trade and other foreign trade. The development of the New England textile industry, for example, was based on a shift of capital from shipbuilding into textiles. Thirdly, the infrastructure developed to serve the import-export trade (banking, insurance, ports, import distribution systems, and internal transportation facilities) was available for subsequent industrial development. Manufacturing developed most rapidly in those industries where imports had been largest. A fourth set of factors relates to the labour supply: the 'ready migration from the farm' in the northeast as a result of the growing difficulties in

44 North, *ibid.*, 166-7 (emphasis in original)

the agricultural sector and the position of the northeastern cities as immigration centres, particularly as regards the destitute Irish who were available at very low wages. Finally, the quality of labour and entrepreneurial talent, as indicated by successes in the adaptation of foreign technology to American conditions and the development of new techniques, was a factor in ensuring that the opportunities presented by the growth of the market were in fact realized by northeastern enterprises.

These are the main factors presented by North, and at least the first four are strikingly similar to those advanced above to explain the position of Montreal. Basically, the explanation lies in the fact that the northeast and Montreal were favoured by prior development based on commerce, as well as by cheap surplus labour from the local agricultural sector and from abroad. When the expansion of a staple product initiated a period of market growth, these regions were best equipped to meet the demand. While the general lines of the explanation are similar, Quebec never occupied the same position in Canada that the northeast occupied in the United States. In 1860 the northeastern United States had 37 per cent of the nation's people and 71 per cent of her manufacturing employment. Ten years later, Quebec had 33 per cent of Canada's population and 35 per cent of manufacturing employment. Thus, while the northeast had four times as much manufacturing employment relative to its population as did the rest of the United States, Quebec's performance differed little from the Canadian average. Several factors account for this very different pattern of regional concentration.

The first element concerns commercial policy. Between 1807 and 1814 American manufacturers enjoyed the natural protection afforded by the disruption of overseas trade, and from 1816 onwards American tariff policy was protectionist. By contrast it was not until 1879 that protection was a clear policy in Canada. In view of Montreal's head start in industrialization, it seems likely that an earlier establishment of protection in Canada would have favoured Quebec over Ontario.[45] Particularly in the key areas of clothing and textiles, which received early protection in the United States and which formed the core of northeastern industry, Montreal merchants, with their superior access to capital and cheap labour, would have been well placed to absorb the major share of any import-substituting industrial development. It has been seen that Montreal's lead over Ontario towns was strongest until about the mid-1850s. Consequently protectionist policies adopted before that date might have enabled Montreal manufacturers to obtain a stronger hold in the young Ontario market, just as was done by New England mills in the American west.

45 I am grateful to Paul Davenport for this point.

A second factor concerns the quality and intensity of the prior development based on commerce. The struggle of Montreal for the trade of the American west is basically a story of failure, and after 1850 Montreal faced a declining share of Ontario's trade as well. By contrast, the cities of the American northeast not only handled the trade of the American (and Canadian) west which had been denied to Montreal, but they also derived even more important benefits from the cotton trade, for which there was no Canadian equivalent. By 1830 forty cents of every dollar received from southern cotton went north in the form of interest, commissions, freight tolls, and insurance. By this time Southerners had more or less abandoned the idea of re-establishing a direct trade with Europe.[46] Consequently, the extent of commerce-based urbanization, capital accumulation, and market growth was much less in Quebec simply because the volume of commercial activity was relatively much less. To the degree that industrial development was based on these factors, the American northeast was in a much stronger position.

A third factor concerns the nature of the market facing eastern manufacturers. It has been seen that the American west of this period followed a pattern of development which bore a close resemblance to that of Ontario, while the northeastern United States and Quebec had several important features in common. The odd man out is obviously the American south, and this region provided the northeast not only with commercial income but also with a large captive market for manufactured goods. For reasons related to the nature of its staple product, the south experienced very limited urban and industrial growth, with the result that many of the linkages flowing from cotton fell to the northeast largely by default. Trade between the north and south was extensive: according to an estimate of 1859, southern raw materials and other produce sent north amounted to $462 million per year, a figure that was balanced by credits to the north consisting of domestic goods valued at $240 million, imports at $106 million, interest brokerage, etc., at $63 million, and southern travellers at $53 million.[47] The south therefore provided a vital market for northern manufactured goods, and this was a positive factor totally absent from the market situation facing the manufacturers of eastern Canada.

It is important to note that these three advantages of the northeast over Quebec (earlier tariffs, more successful commercial development, and a relatively larger national market) do not simply reflect the fact that the United States was larger than Canada. The relations between the northeast and the

46 Cochran and Miller, *Age of Enterprise*, 34.
47 North, *Economic Growth*, 114

TABLE 7.2
Relative regional populations in Canada and the United States, 1850

	Canada			United States
Quebec (= 100)	100	Northeast (= 100)	100
Ontario	107	West	124
		South	67

Source: North, *The Economic Growth of the United States*, 257, and Census of Canada

west were similar to those between Quebec and Ontario, and the relative populations were also similar (Table 7.2). The difference lay in the American south, a region that provided the northeast with a vital source of commercial development and a critical market for manufactured goods. To put the above estimates into perspective, the value of southern produce sent north in 1859 amounted to about seventeen times the gross value of Ontario's record wheat crop reported in the 1860-61 census. If Quebec's prospects for industrial development, relative to its population, were to be equal to the prospects facing the American northeast, one would have to imagine a third Canadian region with a staple export exceeding the value of wheat, with the commercial benefits of that export falling to Quebec, and with a market for manufactured goods that offered very little local resistance to Quebec-produced products. If to these conditions is added the earlier imposition of protective tariffs and the assumption that Ontario wheat and imports flowed through Montreal, then one would have a set of circumstances in which the tariff position, commercial prospects, and national market of Quebec were roughly equivalent (relative to population) to those of the northeastern United States.

It should also be recalled that the northeastern United States was not generally able to retain the natural increase in its population despite the favourable conditions for urban and industrial growth. In five of the six decades between 1800 and 1860 the region experienced a rate of population growth which was less than the rate of natural increase for the country as a whole.[48] The states of southern New England generally showed very low rates of population growth until 1840, after which population growth accelerated.

48 American population figures by state are given in Percy W. Bidwell and John I. Falconer, *History of Agriculture in the Northern United States, 1620-1860* (Washington 1925), 199, 279. Natural rates of increase are from Conrad and Irene B. Taeuber, *The Changing Population of the United States* (New York 1958), 5, 294

Urban growth was able to counteract the rural exodus only after several decades of heavy net out-migration. The situation was more complicated for New York and Pennsylvania, since the western sections of these states were being settled during the first decades of the century while the eastern sections were experiencing net out-migration. If Quebec farmers had been prepared to emigrate in larger numbers, if, for example, Quebec had followed the experience of New England until 1850, then the province's rural population would have been much smaller, and the task of absorbing this population in urban and industrial occupations may have been more manageable in later years. For example, if the population of Quebec had grown at the same rate as that of New England between 1820 and 1850, Quebec's population would have been about 703,000 in 1851, instead of the actual population of 890,000.

In comparison with Quebec, the northeastern United States had both superior opportunities for industrial development and a lower birth rate; yet the region experienced difficulties in retaining its natural population increase. It is hardly surprising, then, that Quebec industry failed to provide enough jobs to absorb the province's rural population.

8
A modified staple approach

The central role accorded to the linkages flowing from Ontario wheat places this work in the tradition of the staple approach to Canadian economic history.[1] On the other hand, I have attempted to deal with two basic issues that are often covered inadequately by the staple approach: first, how does the staple theorist deal with a region that has no staple product; second, how are the linkage effects distributed between the staple-producing region and other regions? Implicitly these issues have been at the heart of the study, as Quebec had no major staple product of its own during most of the period under review, and the major issue was the distribution of the linkages flowing from Ontario wheat between Ontario and Quebec (or, more correctly, Montreal). This chapter begins with an exposition of the modified staple approach implicit in this work, and then applies this framework very briefly to the wheat and oil staples of the prairie provinces.

In the case of a region possessing a staple product, attention focuses first on the properties of that commodity. In the case of a region possessing no staple product, attention focuses on the possibility of appropriating the linkages arising from the staple product of another region. A fundamental proposition of the staple approach is that there must be some external source of demand: the supply of factors of production is not automatically translated into a demand for goods. This external demand may arise directly from the demand for a region's staple product, or indirectly from the demand originating in the staple production of another region. In the case of Quebec, the

1 The main features of the traditional staple approach are described in M.H. Watkins, 'A Staple Theory of Economic Growth,' in W.T. Easterbrook and Watkins, eds., *Approaches to Canadian Economic History* (Carleton Library no 31, 1967), 49-73, and Richard E. Caves, '"Vent for Surplus" Models of Trade and Growth,' in R.E. Baldwin *et al.*, eds., *Trade, Growth and the Balance of Payments* (Chicago 1965), 95-115.

hard facts of continental economics prevented a significant impulse from domestic sources, and the province followed the classic route of regions without their own staple product: it attempted to appropriate the linkages from the staple products of other regions; in particular, it attempted to control the flow of Ontario wheat, and to satisfy the demand for manufactured goods thrown up by the Ontario wheat economy.

The crucial question concerns the conditions under which this attempt will succeed. Given the existence of a staple product and its associated linkages, what determines the division of these linkages between the staple-producing region and other regions? Experience has varied widely, with Ontario retaining a major share of linkages flowing from wheat, while disproportionate shares of the benefits from prairie wheat and from the cotton of the American south, not to mention the primary commodities of many poor countries today, have accrued to other regions.

In dealing with this problem, we begin with the staple product and assess the various linkages flowing from it. The next step is to analyse regional differences in the prior accumulation of population, financial capital, productive capacity, entrepreneurial class, and political power. These factors, which may be designated 'initial endowments' for short, are a legacy of past history. Other things being equal, linkages from a new staple will tend to flow to the region with the greater initial endowment. This may be partly for reasons relating to politcal power, but it is also likely that the economic advantages of larger local markets, more abundant capital, and possibly more advanced technology will confer cost advantages on the better endowed region. The initial endowments, together with the properties of the new staple, will determine the initial distribution of the linkages. As time goes by, the 'flows' of income and population arising from the staple product are added to the 'stocks' of initial endowments. Thus the regional distribution of endowments will itself change over time under the impact of the new staple, and this is likely to cause a continuing change in the regional distribution of the flows.

This formulation implies that while the region with the greater initial endowment certainly has an advantage, relative regional positions are not immutable. Suppose that region A has a greater initial endowment than region B. If the characteristics of the staple are such that region B receives the larger part of the linkages, then the endowment of region B will rise over time relative to the endowment of region A. As this happens, region B's share of the linkages is likely to rise, and eventually the endowments of region B may surpass those of region A. In contrast with theories of 'cumulative causation,' regional differences in aggregate income and population are not bound to widen over time, although, other things being equal, this is likely to occur.

The analysis may also be cast in terms of the principle of comparative advantage. Because of its larger local market and other initial advantages, region A is likely to have a comparative advantage over region B for most manufacturing industries. However, this is only true at the beginning of staple production, for over time comparative advantage will change as the relative endowment of region B rises and as the growing local market of region B permits the economic establishment of additional industries. Thus the approach just outlined is consistent with the principle of comparative advantage when the latter is viewed (as it should be) in a dynamic rather than a static context.

In the Quebec-Ontario case, Ontario wheat created linkages which were distributed between the two provinces in accordance with the forces just outlined. The main factors affecting this distribution were Ontario's access to the American route, the technological bias of the day in favour of the local retention of the linkages from wheat, Montreal's initial position as the commercial centre of Canada, and Quebec's cheap labour. In this case, the flow of linkages from wheat was very large relative to the stock of initial endowments, and Ontario, because it was able to retain key portions of this flow, tended to receive an increasing share of the benefits over time as the centre of income and population shifted westwards. One of the most important aspects of the rising 'endowments' of Ontario was the emergence of an entrepreneurial class that became increasingly independent of Montreal.

The final step in this modified staple approach is to compare the market demand conditions, as determined by the distribution of staple linkages, with the supply conditions as determined by the initial endowments. If demand exceeds supply, there are two extreme possibilities, with reality falling somewhere in the middle. With no mobility of labour or capital, excess demand will raise per capita income in the region, but by assumption there will be no effect on endowments. This case may be ruled out, as changes in endowments lie at the heart of the theory. At the other extreme, factor mobility will ensure the long-run equalization of per capita income across regions, and the only effect of excess demand will be a changing distribution of population. In reality, excess demand will be accompanied by a combination of higher per capita income, higher population, and lower unemployment. The greater the degree of factor mobility, the greater will be the importance of population changes and the less will be the importance of changes in per capita income and unemployment.

Quebec faced the opposite situation, that of the supply of labour exceeding demand. This excess supply was reflected in a combination of the province's low wages, emigration, unemployment, and agricultural underemployment. It could be argued that for social and linguistic reasons Quebeckers were less

TABLE 8.1
The manufacturing sector in the Prairie provinces, selected years, 1890-1976

| | Gross value added in manufacturing ($ millions) | | Population (millions) | | Prairie provinces as percentage of Canada | | |
	Canada	Prairie provinces	Canada	Prairie provinces	Gross value added	Population	Value added per capita
1890	190	5	4.8	0.2	2.5	4.2	60
1910	508	30	7.2	1.3	5.9	18.6	32
1929	1349	101	10.4	2.4	7.5	22.7	33
1956	9542	670	16.1	2.9	7.0	17.7	40
1976	39,874	3289	23.0	3.8	8.2	16.5	50

Source: Census of Canada, Census of Manufacturing

willing than most to emigrate. This may be so, although emigration from the province was nevertheless very substantial. All that can be said with certainty is that the factors analysed in the preceding chapters generated conditions of excess supply, and that factor mobility was not great enough to equalize wages in Ontario and Quebec.

First and foremost, then, this modified staple approach purports to explain regional variations in aggregate income and population. To the extent that mobility is imperfect or to the extent that one region is able to appropriate the economic rent arising from staple production, the theory will also have implications for regional variations in per capita income.

The experience of the prairie wheat economy may be examined in the light of the modified staple approach. Although a full treatment of the subject is beyond the scope of this book, a brief comparison between wheat in Ontario and wheat in the prairies may suggest possible directions for future work. It has been argued that Ontario's wheat staple was the initiating force in the shift of the centre of Canadian population and industry to that province. On the other hand, wheat did not have parallel effects in the Prairie provinces. As indicated in Table 8.1, the wheat boom of the first decade of the twentieth century caused a massive increase in western population and a large but relatively much smaller increase in size of the manufacturing sector. In 1890 per capita value added in manufacturing in the Prairie provinces was 60 per cent of the national average, but it had fallen to 32 per cent of the national average in 1910. This in itself might not be surprising, as it might be reasonable to expect some lag between the wheat boom and associated industrial growth. However, as the table indicates, such a 'filling out' of the manufacturing sector has proceeded at a snail's pace, and not even the advent of Alberta oil after the Second World War has so far been enough to restore the relative position that the prairies held in 1890.

From a static point of view it might simply be argued that the comparative advantage of the Prairie provinces lay in wheat production. It is certainly true that for given levels of population at any one time, the Prairie provinces would devote a high proportion of their human and material resources to wheat production and a low proportion to manufacturing. However, to assume that factors of production are in constant supply is to beg the whole question of economic development. When put in a dynamic context, the relevant question is quite different. Given the massive impulse imparted by the wheat boom, why did population and capital not flow to the region in sufficient quantities to develop a correspondingly large industrial sector based on this initial stimulus? When viewed in this framework, the scope for industrial development is positively, not negatively, related to the initial comparative advantage in wheat. This was certainly the case for Ontario.

The modified staple approach would suggest that we begin by asking two questions: did the difference in initial endowments between the Prairie provinces and central Canada in 1900 exceed that between Ontario and Quebec in 1850; and were the forces that shifted the distribution of endowments in Ontario's favour absent in the case of the prairies?

In answer to the first question, the population of Ontario was 7 per cent greater than that of Quebec in 1850, while the population of Quebec and Ontario combined was more than triple that of the Prairie provinces in 1910. Although Montreal industry was more advanced than Ontario industry in the 1850s, the difference was small compared with the lead of the established industry of central Canada over the prairies in the early twentieth century. Clearly, then, the basic facts of continental settlement patterns resulted in a concentration of population and established industry in Eastern Canada which reduced the prospects for prairie industrialization.

Furthermore, in answer to the second question, the prairies lacked the advantages which had assisted Ontario in its emergence as Canada's industrial heartland. The increasing use of the American trade route as a means by which Ontario towns reduced their dependence on Montreal is in sharp contrast with the monopoly position held by the Canadian Pacific Railway in the Prairie provinces. The small-scale technology of the mid-nineteenth century had served to promote the local retention of staple-related linkages, but by the end of the century larger-scale production and more advanced technology conferred major cost advantages on established industry. In many industries the second half of the nineteenth century was a time of substantial increases in the capital, technology, and organization required to establish a viable enterprise. In such industries Ontario's evolutionary pattern of industrial growth was not open to the prairies at the turn of the century.

Also connected with the larger size of firms was the establishment of branch plants of eastern firms in the west. In industries such as flour milling and agricultural implements, where locational considerations did favour western industry, externally controlled companies were frequently in leading positions from the start. This, it could be argued, retarded the development of an independent entrepreneurial class in the west. While clearly in need of quantification, this brief account does provide some understanding of why the same commodity had such different effects in the Prairie provinces and Ontario. It also serves to underline the inadequacy of explanations based only on the properties of a particular commodity.

Alberta oil is a more recent example of a western staple product. On the basis of the above analysis, the bulk of the proceeds from this product might have been expected to flow eastwards or southwards. The one big contrast between the prairie wheat economy and the prairie oil economy lies in the role of the provincial government. Ontario developed an independent entrepreneurial class gradually as she gained control over the linkages from wheat. By contrast, the relatively low degree of local control over linkages in the prairie wheat economy was associated with a correspondingly weak entrepreneurial class. As emphasized by John Richards and Larry Pratt[2] it would seem that the provincial government is now filling this void, and this fact, together with the government's control over oil rents, may be sufficient to tip the balance in favour of the staple-producing region. If this is correct, the endowments of Alberta will rise over time, and this will tend to shift comparative advantage in manufacturing in favour of that province. In the process, the province's private sector will tend to strengthen, although it would seem that the initial impetus is to be found in the provincial government and the Canadian constitution.

A modified staple approach, therefore, provides a useful analytical framework for explaining regional variations in the growth of aggregate income, population, and, to a lesser extent, per capita income.

---

2 Richards and Pratt, *Prairie Capitalism: Power and Influence in the New West* (Toronto 1979)

9
Merchants and habitants

Historians have tended to blame either the habitants or the Montreal merchants for the economic problems facing nineteenth-century Quebec. According to writers in the tradition of Donald Creighton and Fernand Ouellet, Quebec's agricultural poverty could be ascribed to various shortcomings of the Québécois, aided and abetted by an all-powerful Church. Other writers, notably Tom Naylor, have charged that an anti-industrial bias on the part of the Montreal merchants retarded the province's industrialization, thereby forcing the Québécois to choose between agricultural poverty and emigration.[1]

The comparison between Quebec and the northeastern United States is useful in assessing these two points of view, for it has been seen that the low productivity of Quebec agriculture was due mainly to economic forces operating at the continental level rather than to any special sociological characteristics of the Quebec farmer. By the same token, Quebec's industrial growth, based on commercial capital accumulation followed by the development of large-scale manufacturing catering to a national market, depended on these same economic forces and followed the same lines as in the northeastern United States. The fact that such development was but a pale imitation of the American experience has been ascribed mainly to the narrower range of

---

1 Tom Naylor, *The History of Canadian Business, 1867-1914*, 2 vols. (Toronto 1975). A third hypothesis, that of Albert Faucher and Maurice Lamontagne, 'History of Industrial Development,' in J.-C. Falardeau, ed., *Essais sur le Québec contemporain* (Quebec City 1953), 23-37, is that the lack of iron and coal deposits retarded Quebec's industrialization. Although it has been argued here (pp. 104-7) that this was not a critical factor during the period under discussion, this work shares with Faucher and Lamontagne, and with Faucher, *Québec en Amérique au XIXe siècle* (Montreal 1973), an emphasis on economic factors at the continental level.

opportunities open to Quebec industry, and in particular to the absence of a source of commercial capital and a captive market equivalent to the American south.

Again, then, one is drawn to question explanations based on the special traits of particular social classes. The notion that the agricultural crisis should be ascribed mainly to the social characteristics of the Quebec farmer has been rejected: how could the habitant have been expected to succeed where the much better placed farmer of the northeastern United States had failed? One can view with equal scepticism the hypothesis that Quebec's limited industrial growth was attributable to the anti-industrial and pro-commercial biases of the Montreal merchants: how could Quebec capitalists have provided enough industrial jobs to absorb the surplus agricultural population when northeastern American capitalists, with their superior opportunities and lower population growth, had failed? Just as the Ouellet thesis sets impossible standards of efficiency for the habitant, so the Naylor thesis requires superhuman entrepreneurship on the part of the Montreal merchant. Nineteenth-century Quebec developed along lines that were beyond the control of merchant and habitant alike.

Statistical appendix

TABLE S.1
Western shipments of wheat and flour to Quebec and
exports from Quebec (thousands of bushels)

	Western shipments to Quebec			Exports from Quebec
	From Ontario	From United States	Total	
1817	199	20	219	336
1818	229		229	555
1819	59	19	78	98
1820	168	248	416	536
1821	146	275	421	432
1822	203	123	326	384
1823	201			536
1824	131	109	240	215
1825	177	9	186	918
1826			371	397
1827			627	662
1828			517	296
1829			337	99
1830			931	949
1831			1069	1700
1832				1020
1833			1177	400
1834			400	455
1835			109	350
1836				405
1837				150
1838			644	296
1839			1045	249
1840			2943	1720
1841			3438	2344
1842				1678
1843				1194
1844			3271	2360
1845			3791	2607
1846			4593	3313
1847			5757	3883
1848			4628	2212
1849			4260	2133
1850	3542	87	3629	2139
1851			4312	2079

TABLE S.2
Shipments of wheat and flour by trade route and destination, 1840-51 (thousands of bushels)

	St Lawrence route				American route				Total shipments by ultimate destination				
	Over-seas[a]	Mari-times	Quebec	Total	Over-seas[b]	Mari-times	United States	Total	Over-seas	Mari-times	Quebec	United States	Total
1840	1720		1223	2943					1720		1223		2943
1841	2287	57	1094	3438					2287	57	1094		3438
1842	1598	80							1598	80			
1843	1194								1194				
1844	2262	98	911	3271					2262	98	911		3271
1845	2473	134	1184	3791					2473	134	1184		3791
1846	3138	175	1280	4593					3138	175	1280		4593
1847	3553	330	1874	5757	96		95	191	3649	330	1874	95	5948
1848	1882	330	2416	4628	191	35	1400	1626	2073	365	2416	1400	6254
1849	1738	395	2127	4260	911	20	563	1494	2649	415	2127	563	5754
1850	1434	705	1490	3629	1167	200	1360	2727	2601	905	1490	1360	6356
1851	1304	775	2233	4312	1862	400	36	2298	3166	1175	2233	36	6610

a Includes exports to Maritimes in 1840 and 1843; these overseas exports were overwhelmingly to Britain.
b Includes exports via the Lake Champlain route, which were 56 in 1848, 443 in 1849, 647 in 1850, and 60 in 1851.

TABLE S.3
Gross and net exports of wheat and flour from Ontario, 1850-1871 (millions of bushels)

	Exports of domestic produce						
	Britain via St Lawrence	Maritimes via St Lawrence	Quebec	Via United States	Total	Imports for consumption in Ontario	Net exports
1850	1.4	0.7	1.5	3.2	6.8	0.2	6.6
1851	1.3	0.8	2.2	2.8	7.1	0.3	6.8
1852	1.0	0.7	2.2	4.4	8.2		8.2
1853	1.7	0.9	2.4	4.8	9.8		9.8
1854	0.5	0.7	2.7	4.1	8.2		8.2
1855	0.1	0.4	2.9	7.0	10.4	0.9	9.5
1856	1.5	0.5	2.2	8.9	13.1	1.1	12.0
1857	1.1	0.4	2.4	5.9	9.8	2.5	7.3
1858	1.3	0.5	2.5	4.4	8.7	2.1	6.6
1859	0.3	0.3	2.3	4.0	6.9	1.6	5.3
1860	2.5	0.3	3.0	6.5	12.3	1.5	10.8
1861	6.9	0.5	2.9	7.1	17.4	4.1	13.3
1862	6.1	0.5	3.3	6.1	16.0	6.7	9.3
1863	4.0	0.6	3.3	4.7	12.6	4.5	8.1
1864							
1865	1.4	0.7	3.7	3.9	9.7	3.0	6.7
1866	0.5	0.8	4.2	7.4	12.9	2.0	10.9
1867	0.3	1.8	4.6	4.5	11.2	0.7	10.5
1868	1.4	2.6	4.3	2.2	10.5	2.4	8.1
1869	2.5	2.7	4.3	2.1	11.6	3.0	8.6
1870	3.7	2.6	4.3	1.5	12.1	4.3	7.9
1871	1.3	2.5	4.2	0.9	8.9	3.2	5.7

TABLE S.4
Gross value of agricultural production, Quebec and Ontario, 1851-70 ($ millions current)

| | Ontario | | | Quebec | | |
	1851	1860	1870	1851	1860	1870
Wheat	11.0	32.3	14.2	2.7	3.5	2.1
Hay	7.5	15.3	18.0	8.2	12.3	12.3
Oats	3.1	7.9	7.7	2.4	6.5	5.3
Barley	0.3	1.8	6.6	0.2	1.4	1.2
Potatoes	1.6	4.9	5.1	1.4	4.1	5.4
Peas	1.5	3.6	5.4	0.7	1.0	1.5
Other crops	1.7	5.5	6.8	0.9	1.9	2.7
Total crops	26.7	71.3	63.8	16.5	30.7	30.5
Butter and cheese	2.6	4.9	8.4	1.5	2.8	4.5
Wool	0.7	1.1	1.8	0.4	0.6	0.8
Livestock	6.0	11.9	19.8	3.1	5.8	10.6
Total	36.0	89.2	93.9	21.4	39.9	46.4

TABLE S.5
Estimated agricultural cash income, Quebec and Ontario, 1851, 1860, 1870 ($ millions)

| | 1851 | | 1860 | | 1870 | |
	Quebec	Ontario	Quebec	Ontario	Quebec	Ontario
Wheat		6.5		22.7		6.7
Other	1.2 to	3.7 to	3.4 to	11.3 to	7.4 to	24.7 to
	2.5	5.0	6.9	14.8	11.4	28.7
Total (average)	1.8	10.8	5.2	35.7	9.4	33.4
Occupiers of more than 10 acres (thousands)	71.3	90.2	98.9	127.6	107.6	152.3
Sales per farm ($)	23	125	53	280	87	219
Sales per farm: Quebec as percentage of Ontario	18		19		40	

TABLE S.6

Domestic exports from Quebec and Ontario, 1850-71 (1850-56 £000's; 1857-71 $ millions)

	Forest and ships	Wheat and flour	Other agricultural	Other	Total
1850	1681	954	263	92	2990
1851	1933	843	339	127	3242
1852	1908	1045	436	125	3514
1853	2975	1835	530	163	5503
1854	3047	1724	313	228	5312
1855	2292	2933	724	282	6231
1856	2808	3247	1137	260	7452
1857	13.0	7.3	3.8	1.3	25.4
1858	10.0	5.4	5.1	1.5	22.0
1859	10.1	4.3	6.8	1.9	23.1
1860	11.8	9.5	9.0	2.1	32.4
1861	11.0	14.3	7.7	1.7	34.7
1862	10.5	11.4	7.6	2.2	31.7
1863	15.8	7.9	11.1	2.8	37.6
1864	N/A	N/A	N/A	N/A	N/A
1865	16.2	5.0	13.9	2.8	37.9
1866	15.6	8.3	21.0	3.0	47.9
1867	15.0	8.9	14.0	2.6	40.5
1868	15.3	5.8	13.4	2.3	36.8
1869	16.3	5.1	15.3	2.7	39.4
1870	17.6	6.0	19.2	3.8	46.6
1871	18.8	3.6	18.1	4.4	44.9

TABLE S.7
Industrial working population in Quebec and Ontario, 1851-70 (thousands)

| | Quebec | | | Ontario | | |
	1851	1860	1870	1851	1860	1870
Food	1.4	2.0	2.8	2.5	3.2	5.0
Millers	0.8	0.9	1.5	1.6	2.2	3.5
Bakers	0.6	1.0	1.2	0.5	0.7	1.1
Brewers	0.1	0.1	0.1	0.4	0.4	0.4
Clothing	2.2	4.3	8.2	4.3	5.3	11.1
Textiles	0.3	0.2	0.6	1.8	1.2	2.9
Leather goods	3.9	6.1	8.0	7.3	8.2	9.7
Boots and shoes	3.1	4.9	6.1	5.9	6.3	6.7
Tanners	0.5	0.7	1.2	0.6	0.8	1.0
Metal goods	3.6	5.0	8.0	5.7	8.4	14.7
Blacksmiths	2.8	3.5	4.6	4.2	5.4	7.9
Printers	0.2	0.6	0.9	0.5	1.0	1.8
Wood products	1.2	1.5	2.0	3.8	3.8	5.7
Sawyers	0.4	0.4	0.3	0.9	0.7	1.3
Transportation	0.6	0.7	1.5	1.8	2.3	3.3
Other	1.3	2.1	4.8	3.3	4.6	9.5
Total	14.7	22.7	36.7	31.2	38.1	63.7
Industrial as percentage of total working population	7.2	9.1	10.8	12.6	11.2	13.8

TABLE S.8

Industrial working population in metropolitan and non-metropolitan Quebec and Ontario, 1851-70

	Metropolitan Quebec			Non-metropolitan Quebec			Metropolitan Ontario			Non-metropolitan Ontario		
	1851	1860	1870	1851	1860	1870	1851	1860	1870	1851	1860	1870
Food	320	529	593	1100	1446	2212	324	389	546	2126	2841	4443
Millers	33	94	83	729	849	1390	72	93	144	1509	2115	3328
Bakers	258	372	448	332	583	795	181	224	298	281	429	820
Clothing	1095	2984	4874	1094	1290	3354	1209	1571	3471	3132	3784	7640
Textiles	3	19	15	257	175	561	40	24	48	1798	1185	2847
Leather goods	865	2242	3250	3009	3877	4708	1037	1105	1732	6295	7084	7951
Boots and shoes	726	1954	2663	2343	2962	3399	840	905	1390	5058	5365	5326
Tanners	62	160	356	470	546	820	58	62	82	503	705	915
Metal goods	645	1303	2406	2983	3742	5611	766	1101	3024	4962	7295	11,670
Blacksmiths	264	599	775	2576	2861	3854	287	412	679	3948	5019	7218
Printers	211	564	754	24	78	168	232	501	966	255	480	862
Wood products	563	947	780	623	681	1178	400	384	766	3446	3422	4892
Sawyers	252	200	132	150	177	213	48	35	58	833	701	1210
Transportation	93	136	233	491	547	1263	199	167	305	1590	2100	3038
Other	1026	1885	3122	300	262	1646	1270	1156	2330	2078	3468	7190
Total	4821	10,609	16,027	9881	12,098	20,701	5477	6398	13,188	25,682	31,659	50,533
Industrial as percentage of working population	25.4	26.6	28.0	5.4	5.8	7.3	27.1	24.9	28.4	11.4	10.1	12.1

TABLE S.9
Percentage composition of manufacturing value added in selected regions, 1870

	Metropolitan Quebec	Non-metropolitan Quebec	Metropolitan Ontario	Non-metropolitan Ontario	Montreal	Toronto
Food products	11.5	13.6	14.3	17.2	11.6	18.9
Flour and grist mills	1.3	10.0	1.2	12.3	1.6	1.3
Clothing and textiles	12.5	5.7	11.6	11.1	14.1	12.9
Tailors, etc.	5.1	1.3	8.7	3.5	5.8	10.4
Furriers, etc.	5.7	0.4	1.5	0.2	6.3	1.3
Wool cloth		2.0	0.0	5.3	0.1	
Leather products	25.0	13.4	10.8	10.0	23.4	11.8
Boots and shoes	22.0	4.4	8.4	4.6	21.4	10.3
Transportation equipment	4.7	6.7	2.8	6.1	2.3	1.6
Tobacco working	4.4		1.7	0.2	5.2	2.3
Iron and steel	15.4	13.5	23.0	18.7	16.8	17.5
Blacksmiths	1.1	6.0	0.7	5.4	0.7	0.7
Wood products	6.1	32.1	12.0	21.7	5.7	6.5
Sawmills	0.1	27.9	4.0	14.6	0.9	
Paper products	4.0	2.2	8.3	1.8	3.5	11.1
Chemical products	3.3	3.3	3.6	5.6	3.3	3.3
Crafts (excluding blacksmiths)	4.6	4.3	4.1	1.9	4.7	4.3
Miscellaneous	8.5	5.2	7.7	5.7	9.2	9.9
Total	100.0	100.0	100.0	100.0	100.0	100.0
Total value added (thousands of dollars)	17,310	15,275	12,172	35,300	13,631	5832
Percentage of Quebec and Ontario	21.6	19.1	15.2	44.1	17.0	7.3

TABLE S.10
Per capita value added and productivity and wage rates in eighteen major industries, 1870

	Dollar value			Index (rural Quebec = 100)		
	Per capita value added	Median productivity	Median wage rate	Per capita value added	Median productivity	Median wage rate
Rural Quebec	14.9	345	168	100	100	100
Urban Quebec	103.7	594	259	696	172	154
Rural Ontario	23.7	469	264	159	136	157
Urban Ontario	91.8	570	298	616	165	177

NOTES ON STATISTICS

1 *Ontario shipments of wheat and flour* (Figures 2.1, 2.2, 2.3, and 2.4)

Tables S.1, S.2, and S.3 provide the basic data from which Figures 2.1 and 2.2 and portions of Figures 2.3 and 2.4 are derived. For all tables, flour is converted to wheat on the basis of one barrel of flour equal to five bushels of wheat.

TABLE S.1
Sources are as follows:
(a) *Western shipments:*
1817-23: *Journals of the Legislative Assembly of Lower Canada* (JLALC), 1823-24, vol. 33, app. W
1824: JLALC, 1825, vol. 34, app. T
1825: JLALC, 1826, vol. 35, app. U
1826-29: JLALC, 1830, vol. 39, app. D
1830: JLALC, 1831, vol. 40, app. G
1831: JLALC, 1831-32, vol. 41, app. Q
1832: JLALC, 1834, vol. 43, app. E
1834: JLALC, 1835, vol. 44, app. F
1835: JLALC, 1835-36, vol. 45, app. Q
1838: *Journals of the Legislative Assembly of Canada* (JLAC), 1841, app. EE
1839-41: JLAC, 1842, app. F
1844-50: I.D. Andrews, *Report on the Trade, Commerce, and Resources of the British North American Colonies* ... United States Senate, 31st Congress, 2nd session, executive document no 23 (Washington 1851), 277-8, 286-7, 289

1851: I.D. Andrews, *Report on the Trade and Commerce of the British North American Colonies and upon the Trade of the Great Lakes and Rivers*, 32nd Congress, 1st session, executive document no 136 (Washington 1853), 438

(b) *Exports:*

1817-30: H.A. Innis and A.R.M. Lower, *Select Documents in Canadian Economic History, 1783-1885* (Toronto 1933), 265-6

1831-37: Fernand Ouellet, *Histoire économique et sociale du Québec, 1760-1850* (Montreal 1971), 609

1838-39: Andrews (1851), 180

1840-52: as for Table S.2

TABLE S.2

For 1840-47 the sum of the first two columns is equal to total exports as reported by Andrews (1851), 180, and in Table S.1. These figures are virtually identical to those of H.Y. Hind *et al.*, *Eighty Years' Progress of British North America* (Toronto 1863), 291, as reprinted in Innis and Lower, *Select Documents*, 266. For 1848-49 the sum of exports to the Maritimes and overseas is again taken from Andrews (1851), 180, but exports via Lake Champlain have been added. These were obtained as follows: 1848 – Andrews (1851), 232; 1849 – JLAC, 1850, app. HH; 1850-51 – Andrews (1853), 413. Prior to these dates, exports via this route appear to have been negligible – JLAC, 1846, app. GG, JJJ. For 1850-51 exports from Quebec City and Montreal were obtained from Andrews (1853), 413; these figures are very close to those of Hind, *ibid.*, 291, until 1849, from which time Hind's figures represent total exports. For the total period the largest discrepancy is less than 7 per cent of exports. Exports to the Maritimes in 1841 and 1842 are from JLAC, 1842, app. F. Figures for St Lawrence and bonded exports to the Maritimes in later years are from Andrews (1853), 414, 435. The figures for shipments by the American route are probably severely understated, particularly in 1848 and 1849. Totals are from Andrews (1851), 180, 188, 239, 242, and Andrews (1853), 413. In all cases, shipments via Lake Champlain have been subtracted. For the distribution between bonded wheat and wheat sold for US consumption, for 1851 the source was Andrews (1853), 413, and for 1850 the distribution was calculated from Andrews (1851), 48. For 1849 it was assumed that Canadian bonded wheat received in New York City was the total of bonded wheat received – Andrews (1853), 433. R.L. Jones, *History of Agriculture in Ontario, 1613-1880* (Toronto 1946), 177-8, stated that in 1848, 1,400,000 bushels of wheat were bought in Toronto by Oswego and Rochester millers, and this figure was used for American consumption, leaving only 190,000 for export in bond. The small amount in 1847 was arbitrarily divided equally between the two categories – see *ibid.*, 172. It seems obvious that there is considerable understatement: for example, while

New York was by no means the only recipient of bonded wheat, receipts at that city are stated at 1.4 million bushels of Canadian wheat and flour in 1849, 3.2 million in 1850, and 3.1 million in 1851. These figures are a total of 1.2 million bushels greater than *total* recorded exports to the United States in these years and this is before taking account of domestic exports such as those cited by Jones and of other cities receiving bonded wheat. Nevertheless, so as not to overstate the case, the low figures have been retained. The figures for Quebec are the difference between total shipments to Montreal as derived already (fourth column from the left) and exports from Quebec (the first two columns).

TABLE S.3
The Trade and Navigation Returns provide figures on exports of domestic produce and imports for home consumption. The export figures give the Canadian port of origin, the country of destination, and the volume and value of exports. Parallel information is provided for imports. Tonnage figures are provided for shipments by the various canals, with distinctions made between American and British (that is, Canadian) points of origin and destination. All information is provided for both wheat and flour.

Exports to Britain and the Maritimes via the St Lawrence and total exports via the United States are taken directly from the trade returns. The trade returns add 20 per cent to exports from inland ports to allow for undercoverage, and this procedure has been adopted. Initially it was intended to use figures based on shipments by the St Lawrence canals to estimate Quebec consumption. However, this method proved to be impossible because of problems relating to re-exports and the increasing use of the Grand Trunk for the transportation of flour. The method adopted was first to assume a per capita annual Quebec consumption of six bushels. For the census years, Quebec production was subtracted from the implied total provincial consumption to determine total net imports from Ontario and the United States. Imports to Quebec ports from the United States were subtracted from this figure to provide an estimate of imports from Ontario. It is possible that a portion of the imports from the United States to Ontario ports was shipped to Quebec. This would reduce estimated Ontario sales to Quebec and imports for Ontario consumption by equal amounts, so that there would be no effect on total net exports from Ontario. Similar remarks apply to the possibility that some Quebec-produced wheat was exported (that is, sales of Ontario wheat would be higher in Quebec and lower in export markets). For intercensal years, it was assumed that Quebec population and wheat production followed even trends. The results are not sensitive to this assumption in view of the low rate of growth of population and the low level of wheat production in all three years (3.1, 2.7, and 2.1 million bushels in 1851, 1860, and 1870 respectively).

The results of these calculations are highly consistent with census figures on Ontario wheat production. The only important assumption is the level of per capita consumption of wheat in Quebec. If consumption were five bushels instead of six bushels, net exports of Ontario wheat would be reduced by about one million bushels annually (that is, by an average of slightly more than 10 per cent of the estimated amounts). A five-bushel consumption level must be regarded as an absolute minimum, given the estimated levels in the years before 1850, the greater prosperity after 1850, and the very high income elasticity of demand for wheat at low levels of consumption.

Figures apply to calendar years between 1850 and 1863 and to years ending 30 June for 1865 and subsequent years. Numbers are provided for all periods except the first six months of 1864. The figures for 1850 and 1851 are taken from Table S.2 (the small difference in the case of exports via the United States reflects the addition of 20 per cent for undercoverage for Table S.2 but not for Table S.1). The price of wheat plotted in Figure 2.3 is equal to the value of Canadian wheat exports divided by the number of bushels.

FIGURE 2.4

In addition to figures on net exports of wheat and flour, Figure 2.4 is based on estimates of total wheat production, wheat consumption by the agricultural and non-agricultural sectors, and the value of all exports from Ontario.

Estimates of wheat consumption are based on a per capita annual consumption figure of six bushels, which is the upper limit of the estimate contained in the 1851 census. For census years, the reported production figures were very close to the figures estimated by adding consumption at six bushels per capita to the figures for net exports. Population was assumed to rise at an even rate in the inter-censal years. For reasons discussed below (pp. 138-40) the ratio of the farm to non-farm population was assumed to fall evenly from 67 per cent in 1850 to 57 per cent in 1871, and it was assumed that per capita annual consumption was six bushels for both groups.

Ontario exports consisted of (a) net and gross exports of wheat and flour as previously calculated; (b) direct exports of other commodities from Ontario ports as reported in the Trade and Navigation Returns; and (c) indirect exports from Ontario (that is, exports that went via Quebec, and hence were recorded as Quebec exports). The major commodities in the latter group were other grains, dairy products, and wood products. Based on a detailed examination of these commodities in McCallum, 'Agriculture and Economic Development in Quebec and Ontario to 1870,' PHD thesis, McGill University, 1977, pp. 402-6, it was assumed that Ottawa Valley (Ontario) exports via Montreal averaged $3.5 million per year, and that other (mainly agricultural) indirect exports via Montreal rose from $500,000 per year in the first half of the 1850s to $4 million by 1871.

2 Quebec wheat deficit/surplus (Figure 3.1)

For 1792-1812 the figures are exports from Quebec taken from Innis and Lower, *Select Documents*, 265. For 1813-16, 1823, and 1834-37, the figures are from Ouellet, *Histoire économique et sociale*, 609. For the remaining years the figures are from Tables S.1 and S.2. Imports through St-Jean have not been included. If they had been, the deficits would have been higher, but the trade returns indicate that these imports were not very significant. The largest quantity seems to have been 85,000 bushels in 1841 – JLAC, 1843, app. SS – with other years very much smaller. The figures are generally equal to the difference between western shipments and exports, with the exception of certain years in the 1830s when wheat was imported from Europe.

3 Gross value of agricultural production (Table S.4)

Volumes of production of field products, wool, butter, cider, and cheese were taken from the censuses. For 1870 prices were generally taken from the Department of Agriculture, *Monthly Bulletin of Agricultural Statistics*, May 1921. For 1851 and 1860 prices were generally taken from K.W. Taylor and H. Mitchell, *Statistical Contributions to Canadian Economic History* (Toronto 1931). For a few minor products, prices were not available from one or both of these sources, and in such cases prices were taken from the 1851 census. The vegetable products price index contained in Taylor and Mitchell was applied to these prices to provide estimates for the other two years.

For horses, annual domestic sales were estimated at half the stock of horses in Montreal and Quebec City for Quebec. The ratio of Ontario population to Quebec population was applied to this figure to provide an estimate for Ontario. The increase in stock was estimated on the assumption that the change in stock between census dates was spread evenly over the nine years between 1851 and 1860 and the ten years between 1860 and 1870. Finally, exports, which formed the major component of horse sales, were added to the domestic figures. For domestic sales and stock increases, price was based on that contained in the 1851 census, together with the price index of animal products contained in Taylor and Mitchell. The values of horse exports were taken from the Trade and Navigation Returns. For sheep, cattle, and pigs, it was assumed that the ratio of animals killed on the farm or sold to total stock for 1870 also applied in the two earlier years. Prices and stock increases were derived in the same way as for horses.

4 *Agricultural cash income* (Table S.5 and Figure 4.1)

For wheat, it was assumed that cash sales were equal to the value of production, less 5½ bushels per member of the farm population, less 1½ bushels per acre for seeding. It was assumed that the farm population as a percentage of the total was 67 in 1851, 62 in 1860, and 57 in 1870. Net sales for Quebec were regarded as zero, although the above calculation yields negative numbers.

For other commodities, two methods of calculation were used, and the results of Figure 4.1 represent the average of the two methods. In both cases exports to the United States were assumed to originate in the province of export. In dealing with overseas exports and domestic sales, the first method allocated sales of each commodity by province in proportion to production in each province, while the second method allocated sales in such a way that per capita consumption of each commodity was the same in the agricultural sectors of both provinces. The first method represents an overstatement of Quebec's contribution, and the second method is an understatement to the extent that food consumption levels were higher among Ontario farmers than among Quebec farmers. Based on the relative size of the agricultural and urban populations, the importance of imports, the requirements of the forestry sector, and the degree of self-sufficiency on the part of non-farm rural and urban families, it was assumed that domestic cash sales as a percentage of production minus exports were as follows (percentages):

	1851	1860	1870
Hay and oats	8	8	8
Potatoes and peas	10	12.5	15
Other crops	15	17.5	20
Butter and cheese	10	20	30
Wool	10	15	20
Livestock	10	20	30

Further details concerning the basis of these percentages are given in McCallum, 'Agriculture and Economic Development,' 224-8.

5 *Exports from Quebec and Ontario* (Table S.6 and Figure 4.2)

Figures are from the Trade and Navigation Returns. They apply to calendar years until 1863, after which they apply to years ending 30 June. Exports of bullion, re-exports, and estimated undercoverage at inland ports are excluded.

6 *Industrial statistics* (Tables S.7 to S.10)

The figures are all from the decennial censuses of 1851, 1860, and 1870. All three censuses contain information on occupational structure, but usable information on value added is contained only in the 1870 census. Industrial working population has been defined to include blacksmiths but not construction trades, a procedure that has also been followed for the figures on value added. As noted in the text, for reasons of data availability, metropolitan Quebec is defined as Montreal and Quebec City, and metropolitan Ontario is defined as Toronto, Hamilton, Kingston, London, and Ottawa. The remainder of each province is designated non-metropolitan.

With respect to Table S.10, as indicated on p. 86 (n6), median productivity and wage rates are based on the twenty-three industries which employed over 1000 people in one province and at least 500 in the other province. For the regional medians, the same twenty-three industries were examined, but five were eliminated because production was insignificant in at least one of the four regions. The measures of productivity and wage rates have two drawbacks. First, aggregate value added and wages were divided by total employment, although not all workers were employed for the same length of time. However, there seems to be no reason to believe that this would bias the comparison between the two provinces. The second factor is that the composition of the labour force varied. However, it was possible to determine the approximate age-sex composition of the industrial labour force (coverage is over 90 per cent), as indicated in the following figures (percentages):

	Quebec	Ontario
Males older than 16	74	79
Females older than 16	15	12
Males and females younger than 16	11	8

All other things being equal, this implies that if women and children were paid half what men were paid, the mean wage rate would be 2.3 per cent higher in Ontario than in Quebec as a result of this factor alone.

7 *Occupational structure*

The census figures relating to the relative importance of the farm population were as follows (percentage distribution of working population):

	Quebec			Ontario		
	1851	1860	1870	1851	1860	1870
Agricultural class	38.6	43.3	47.1	35.2	39.5	49.4
Domestic class	8.4	8.0	6.2	7.3	6.4	5.8
Unclassified	33.3	20.4	15.5	32.8	29.2	14.7
Sub-total	80.3	71.7	68.8	75.3	75.1	69.9
Other	19.7	28.3	31.2	24.7	24.9	30.1
Total	100.0	100.0	100.0	100.0	100.0	100.0

It is clear that classifications changed over time and that the key factor is the composition of the unclassified group. This group, consisting almost entirely of 'labourers,' appears to have been treated in two different ways by other authors. For Canada as a whole, O.J. Firestone, 'Development of Canada's Economy, 1850-1900,' in National Bureau of Economic Research, *Studies in Income and Wealth*, XXIV (1960), 245, concluded that, for 1851, 55 per cent of the unclassified group were farm labourers. He based this figure on the occupational classification of the 1870 census, but at least in the absence of further information it is difficult to see how the 1870 census would help in this regard, particularly in light of the 15 per cent unclassified in that year. Maurice Séguin, *La nation 'canadienne' et l'agriculture* (Trois-Rivières 1970), 73-4, dealing with Quebec, simply regarded all the labourers as 'fils de cultivateurs' and classified them as agricultural.

Séguin's position, while undoubtedly extreme, gains some support from an inspection of the distribution of 'labourers' among the towns and counties of the two provinces. Relative to population, they are remarkably evenly distributed in both provinces and in all three years, with one significant exception. The major towns had only about half the 'labourers' that would be expected on the basis of population alone. This suggests that the labourers were not primarily engaged in urban activities such as manufacturing. Furthermore, there is no particular concentration in eastern Ontario or western Quebec, as would be expected if the timber trade were primarily responsible, and the even distribution rules out a significant contribution from major public works. They were not artisans or craftsmen because these groups were classified in minute detail. Thus, by a process of elimination and on the basis of the even distribution, it seems likely that most of the labourers were either farmers' sons or seasonal or full-time farm labourers. If, say, three-quarters of the unclassified group is assumed to be in agriculture, and if the domestic class is omitted from the computation, then the ratio of farm to total working population falls from 69 per cent in 1850 to 63 per cent in 1870 for Quebec, while the ratio remains steady at about 65 per cent for Ontario. Exclusion of the domestic class is justified not only because much of it would have been on farms but also because it consists mainly of female servants, whereas only males are included in the figures for agriculture and for the unclassified group.

These figures, albeit very approximate, receive support from other quarters. In the United States, 65 per cent of the working population was said to be agricultural in 1850. H.C. Pentland, 'Labour and the Development of Industrial Capitalism in Canada,' PHD thesis, University of Toronto, 1960, pp. 148-9, estimated that perhaps 80 per cent of the French population was engaged in agriculture throughout the nineteenth century. In 1850 the non-French population made up 25 per cent of the total, and just over 20 per cent of this group lived in Montreal and Quebec City. If we suppose (conservatively) that one-half of the non-French group outside the major cities was engaged in agriculture, then Pentland's 80 per cent estimate implies that 70 per cent of the total population was in agriculture. Séguin, *La nation 'canadienne,'* 73-4, arrives at a figure of 75 to 80 per cent for Quebec in 1851 by including labourers and male servants outside Montreal and Quebec City and by adding about two-thirds of the excess of 'occupiers of land' over 'farmers.' This latter procedure is questionable, since he has classified two-thirds of those occupying ten acres or less as farmers; but, on the other hand, he apparently did not correct for the downward bias created by the inclusion of all 11,000 female servants in the non-agricultural working population.

As for the ratio before 1850, Séguin, 74, estimated that Quebec's rural population made up 85 per cent of the total in 1820, and William Evans, *Supplementary Volume to a Treatise on the Theory and Practice of Agriculture* (Montreal 1836), 72, stated that 85 per cent of the population of Quebec 'belong exclusively to the agricultural class.' Given the approximate nature of all these figures, it seems reasonable to speak of an agricultural population making up roughly three-quarters of the total before 1850, perhaps two-thirds by the middle of the century, and three-fifths by 1870. These orders of magnitude would apply to both provinces, but it should also be noted that some 3 to 10 per cent of the farmers and farm workers of Quebec received a supplement to their incomes by working in shipbuilding or as shantymen and raftsmen in the timber trade.

Subject index

Index of authors cited

Numbers refer to the first page on which the work is cited.

The State and Economic Life series

EDITORS: Mel Watkins, University of Toronto; Leo Panitch, Carleton University

This series serves as a vehicle for the publication of original studies in the general area of Canadian political economy and economic history, with particular emphasis on the part played by the government in shaping the economy. Collections of shorter studies, as well as theoretical or internationally comparative works, may also be included.

1 The State and Enterprise:
   Canadian Manufacturers and the Federal Government, 1917-1931
   by TOM TRAVES

2 Unequal Beginnings:
   Agriculture and Economic Development in Quebec and Ontario until 1870
   by JOHN McCALLUM